Wonderful Worship
in Smaller Churches

Wonderful Worship
in Smaller Churches

David R. Ray

The Pilgrim Press
Cleveland, Ohio

The Pilgrim Press, Cleveland, Ohio 44115
www.pilgrimpress.com
© 2000 by David R. Ray
All rights reserved. Published 2000

Grateful acknowledgment for permission to reprint from the following: T. S. Eliot, "Choruses from 'The Rock'" in *Collected Poems 1909–1962*. Copyright © 1936 Harcourt, Inc.; copyright © 1964, 1963 T. S. Eliot.•Lyle Schaller, *Looking in the Mirror: Self-appraisal in the Local Church*. Copyright © 1984 Abingdon Press.

Printed in the United States of America on acid-free paper

05   04   03   02   01   5   4   3   2

Library of Congress Cataloging-in-Publication Data
Ray, David R., 1942–
    Wonderful worship in smaller churches / David R. Ray.
        p.   cm.
    ISBN 0-8298-1400-0 (pbk. : alk. paper)
        1. Small churches.   2. Worship.   I. Title.
BV637.8 .R395   2000
264—dc21

00-051648

CONTENTS

PREFACE

It was not because you were more numerous than any other
people that the Lord set his heart on you and chose you—for
you were the fewest of all peoples. It was because the Lord loved
you and kept the oath that he swore to your ancestors.
—Deuteronomy 7:7–8

n addition to my parents, smaller churches have made me who I am.
They have called me by name, nurtured me, loved me, tolerated me,
taught me the faith, called me to ministry, taught me to be a leader, accepted my faults, given me an arena in which to apply my gifts, and made me
feel at home. My personal hall of heroes is peopled with names like Ruby,
Chuck, Bud, Paul, Carl and Rotha, Judy, Red and Francis, Keith and Judy,
Margee and Bob, John and Jean, and many, many others. To the churches where
I've sojourned, from Massachusetts to California, and to all the people who are
responsible for my better qualities, have forgiven my lesser qualities, and have
given me opportunities for ministry, I feel profound gratitude. I dedicate this
book to all of them and to the people like them who will read this book.

I've spent thirty years as pastor of four remarkable churches. They were
amazingly different from one another except that all were small churches with
an average worship attendance ranging from twenty to seventy. I was pastor of
the Trinitarian Congregational Church in the tiny, blue collar, hill town of
Warwick, Massachusetts, from 1971 to 1985. I served four-year pastorates in
rural Shrewsbury, Vermont, and in Emmetsburg, Iowa, a declining county seat
town of four thousand. Since 1993, I've been pastor of the urban First Congregational Church of San Rafael, California, a few miles north of San Francisco
and the county seat for one of the wealthiest, most secular, and beautiful counties in America. Each of these churches had been in serious decline for decades.
Each of these churches experienced significant transformation during my pas-
torate. Membership, involvement, and worship attendance grew steadily; financial resources grew annually; morale shot up and stayed up; and each developed
a serious mission commitment. What accounted for the dramatic reversal in
each church?

It was not because I have a gregarious, magnetic personality. I don't. It was not because I knocked on ten doors every week. I'm too shy and didn't have time due to my other bivocational commitments. It was not because I'm a charismatic preacher. I'm not. It was not because there was dramatic growth in the community around us. There wasn't. It was not because each community was undergoing a spiritual revival. Far from it.

I believe the spiritual and organizational transformation in these very diverse churches was due to four factors:

1. The set of understandings and principles that govern how I do ministry and provide leadership in smaller churches.
2. My love for each church.
3. The worship shared within them.
4. My commitment to two essential assumptions about smaller churches.

What are the two assumptions? In 1982, Lyle Schaller and I each published books about small churches. He wrote *The Small Church Is Different*, and I wrote *Small Churches Are the Right Size*. These two fundamental understandings—that small churches are different and that small churches are the right size—should be tattooed on the left and right arm of every denominational leader and every pastor and lay leader of a small church. They are fundamentally true and make all the difference in whether or how a smaller church is faithful and effective.

First, Schaller understood that size determines the nature of every organization; therefore, small churches behave differently and must be understood and led differently than churches of other sizes. Secondly, I understood that by biblical, theological, and functional criteria, small churches are the right size to be and do everything God expects a church to be and do—without excuse and without apology. While they may have challenges, they also have size-related advantages in being and doing all that God requires.

When I wrote *Small Churches Are the Right Size*, based on ten years of ministry in Warwick and extensive study of the literature and learnings about smaller churches, I defined small churches by ten characteristics which I have since expanded to twenty-seven. Because they are fundamentally essential for understanding all aspects of smaller churches—including how they worship—here is a complete listing of characteristics of small churches:

1. A small church fulfills the expectations of its people.
2. Everyone knows, or thinks they know, everyone or almost everyone else.
3. Beyond knowing one another, small churches act like *family*.
4. In a small church, almost everyone feels that they are important and needed.

5. In small churches, organizational functioning is simple rather than complex, and they can decide and act as a whole rather than in subgroups and committees.
6. Communication is rapid.
7. Small churches are known by their distinctive personalities more than their organized programs.
8. They're likely to be rooted in their history and nervous about their future.
9. A small church's theology is real, personal, horizontal, and historical; not systematic, vertical, or ethereal.
10. A small church understands mission and prefers to do mission in personal, pragmatic, and immediate ways.
11. A small church wants its minister to be a pastor, friend, and generalist; not a professional, specialist, administrator, or chief executive officer.
12. The New Testament church is the model or paradigm of a small church.
13. Small churches are people oriented, not goal or future oriented.
14. Small churches are more likely to laugh, cry, flare up—be emotional.
15. **Worship is their primary activity.**
16. Eating together is their favorite activity.
17. Small churches are more story than treatise; more myth than method.
18. They operate on fluid, people time.
19. Most small church people want a say in how their money is spent and would rather give what's needed, when needed, and usually privately.
20. Lay people are more important to their long range survival than their pastor is; the pastor may be critical for their long-range flourishing.
21. It is difficult to become part of a small church, and more difficult to get out of one.
22. Small churches are tough and resilient.
23. Small churches would rather do it *our way*.
24. They're more effective than they are efficient.
25. Small churches prefer and are better at special events than long-term programs.
26. They're better at meeting immediate needs than long-range planning.
27. Small churches are locally owned and operated.

The more closely these characteristics fit a church, the smaller it is—in style if not in numbers. (For more information on these characteristics, refer to my book, *The Big Small Church Book* [Cleveland: The Pilgrim Press, 1992].)

ONE

INTRODUCTION TO WORSHIP

What life have you if you have not life together?
There is no life that is not in community,
And no community not lived in praise of God.

. . .

And now you live dispersed on ribbon roads,
And no man knows or cares who is his neighbor
Unless his neighbor makes too much disturbance,
But all dash to and fro in motor cars,
Familiar with the roads and settled nowhere.[1]

These prophetic lines are about the human condition, not about going to church. The poet, T. S. Eliot, writing in the middle of the twentieth century, concludes that contemporary times are times of isolation and alienation. What was true in 1950 is even more true at the beginning of the new millennium. Consider the way life is for many, if not most of us. We shop for wants and needs at Wal-Mart rather than the Main Street variety store where we run into our neighbors. We buy foods from around the world at the supermarket rather than locally grown produce at the corner grocery. We are cogs in the multinational corporation work force instead of valued employees of the locally owned company. We seek entertainment and communication face-to-screen rather than face-to-face. We substitute virtual reality for reality itself. Increasingly, seekers browse at the electronic or mega church rather than committing themselves to participation at their neighborhood church where they are known and needed. Should we be surprised that these cultural changes change us? Why then are we surprised that economic disparity, emotional stress and illness, family and community disintegration, and acts of aggression are growing?

Eliot implies that familiarity with roads have replaced familiarity with one another. (If Eliot were writing this poem today, he might have substituted the personal computer and other technologies as threats to personal interaction and relationship.) He suggests that life full of gadgetry and advancement is no replacement for life together. He understands that life in mere proximity to one another does not substitute for life lived and invested in community. He believes that life in community, where life in its fullness is realized, doesn't reach fruition outside of life in relation to the God of Love.

I believe there is no more crucial imperative for Western civilization at the beginning of the twenty-first century than Eliot's pronouncement that "there is no life that is not in community and no community not lived in praise of God." If one agrees with this conviction, then worshiping congregations small enough to foster and experience genuine community in their intimate, communal praise of God are not an anachronism but a life-saving oasis in an arid desert of isolation and alienation. Building on this foundation, the purpose of this book is not to merely help rehabilitate our Sunday religious gatherings, but to help smaller churches realize and maximize the full potential of their worship in order to create the essential community of God for all God's people.

I'm just enough of an anthropologist to be intrigued by the fact that virtually every culture since humans exited the caves has come together for a variety of religious rituals. Either these were exercises in primitive folly or the whole of human history has understood that there is no meaning and structure in our living without religious ritual to realize that meaning and structure. Either all of human ancestry has been motivated by superstition and delusion or most of humanity in every age has responded to a genuine spiritual hunger out of a genuine spiritual need. Tom Driver, in *Liberating Rites*, asks, "is it not odd that human beings, in all societies, everywhere and in all ages, have engaged in the making and performing of rituals? Why have they done this, when life is full of dangers and challenges that would seem to require more practical kinds of activity? . . . Indeed, they seem to be born out of necessity."[2]

Throughout history, most cultures have had established rituals for seasonal events like planting and harvesting, initiating the newborn, coming of age, forming families, coping with crisis, and dying. We've had them in our own Judeo-Christian traditions from our beginnings. Such religious rituals punctuate our scriptures from Genesis to Revelation. Yet these rituals lose their life when they become ritual for ritual sake or when humans, out of their perceived self-sufficiency, forget their need for ritual. Whichever is the case, the loss of living ritual leads to loss of meaningful life and a breakdown in societal interdependence and health.

Psalm 122 describes what Judeo-Christian people have done for thousands of years: "I was glad when they said to me, 'Let us go to the house of the Lord!' . . . To it the tribes go up . . . to give thanks to the name of the Lord." We've been going to holy places and gatherings for eons—sometimes with passion and power, sometimes merely with perfunctory mumbles. Perhaps you and I, the reader and writer, can achieve more of the former and less of the latter.

This book will be using throughout three closely related and overlapping words—*ritual, liturgy,* and *worship.*

RITUAL

Ritual is a historic term for worship that means different things to different people. For some church attendees, it implies an empty, repetitious religious practice. Anthropologists use the term to describe a culture's ancient practices which carry and express the essence of that culture. Liturgists and academics use ritual to mean those worship practices that have become established through repetition, like praying the Lord's Prayer and sharing the Lord's Supper.

Two books about ritual offer particularly profound insights. In his winsome and provocative style, Robert Fulghum, in *From Beginning to End: The Rituals of Our Lives*, discusses the role rituals (religious, cultural, and personal) play in defining and fulfilling our lives. He writes: "From beginning to end, the rituals of our lives shape each hour, day, and year. Everyone leads a ritualized life. Rituals are repeated patterns of meaningful acts."[3] Fulghum understands that rituals are neither dead customs from the past nor printed rites in a prayer book or hymnal. Rather, they are the select acts, out of the various random actions of our lives, that become customary and efficacious because they mean more than they are. On one level, the ritual of the first cup of coffee in the morning means far more than a shot of cobweb-clearing caffeine. On another level, the Lord's Supper means far more to the frequent practitioner than ingesting a bit of bread and sip of juice. An action becomes ritual when it uncovers, expresses, and captures a deeper and broader meaning. For the practitioner of religious ritual, Fulghum's book is a refreshing exploration of the many ways rituals color and texture our lives.

Tom Driver's book, *Liberating Rites*, is a scholarly anthropological and theological examination of the role of ritual in forming, sustaining, and transforming cultures and religions. He confesses at first that ritual has not always intrigued him. At one time he found it a dreary subject. At another time he viewed ritual with suspicion, as the esoteric and irrational practices of people more primitive than learned. With many others, he felt that rituals were routine acts repeated to the point of boredom. Then Driver discovered the transformative power of ritual—both historically and currently—to form, sustain, and transform life.

Driver agrees with the claim of a women's group that: "ritual is the license we give one another and God to don bright colors and move in circles and claim this moment as *a kairos*. Only where there is death does ritual cease. Without it we literally die."[4] Driver rejects the notion that rituals are practices humans freely choose to invent. Looking back with the eye of an anthropologist, he sees more evidence that people have been shaped by unavoidable rituals than that they have rationally created them. He says, "It is not as true to say that we human beings invented rituals as that rituals have invented us."[5]

He believes that rituals accomplish three major functions: making and preserving order, fostering community, and effecting transformation. Ritual is crucial in building the vitality of our groups, in maintaining order in the face of anarchy, in building a sense of community instead of splintering individualism, and in enabling the transformation of persons and groups rather than settling for the status quo. The size of a group helps or hinders a ritual's effort to preserve order, foster community, and effect transformation.

Driver understands the dynamic relationship between religion and ritual. He perceives that both God and humans depend on ritual. Humans experience ritual as a medium through which the Spirit or the Holy is revealed and communicates. Less obvious, but just as real, the Holy depends on ritual as the vehicle through which it will be discerned and experienced on the human level. Even Jesus used religious ritual for self-revelation. He began his ministry by reading from the Isaiah scroll during synagogue worship to announce that: "today this scripture has been fulfilled in your hearing" (Luke 4:21). He ended his ministry by celebrating the Passover ritual with his little church of apostles in a borrowed room. He injected new meaning into the ancient seder ritual and prescribed: "Do this in memory of me" (Luke 22:19). We still do.

Carl Dudley in an article in *Christian Ministry* named three essential dimensions of ritual. First, ritual is more physical than mental. Rituals are not simply mental exercises. They are things we do, often dramatically. They include and often focus on physical objects such as water, bread and chalice, money, flowers, rings, and other commonly accepted symbols.

Second, ritual is more communal than personal. While a couple is legally married when the officiant signs the wedding license, they are really wed when vows are exchanged and sealed with a kiss in front of their invited witnesses. As a wet behind the ears seminarian, I suggested that the minister marrying my bride and me serve the two of us communion as part of the ceremony. Wiser than I, he refused unless it was served to all those present. Rituals are primarily corporate, not private, events.

Third, ritual liberates those in worship to see within and beyond themselves. Our brains can only process so much. When our brain is coupled with our heart and the rest of our senses, we can process much more. In the same way, rituals are enhanced and made real when they incorporate mind and heart, sight, sound, smell, and touch.[6] Among the many gifts worship offers the worshiper is the rediscovery of the power of rituals in enriching and transforming our lives.

LITURGY

The word liturgy gets little more respect than ritual in common parlance. For many, it's synonymous with "smells and bells," or conjures up memories of dry routine. A common, but incomplete, understanding of liturgy is that it is a fixed form of public worship. These perceptions barely scratch the surface. Liturgy is far more than games we play on Sunday morning. Through word, symbol, and memory, liturgy has the power to move us beyond our static reality. Liturgy can help us recall what we have forgotten. It gives words to feelings and substance to the poorly articulated. It can give joyful harmony to joyful noises. It can begin healing a grieving heart. It can transform a collection of individuals into a community of believers. To understand liturgy, we need to understand what it is and who does it.

Faith is given form with both structures and words. Two travelers were admiring the beautiful cathedral in Amiens, France. One asked, "Why can't we build piles like this any more?" The other answered, "In those days people had convictions. We moderns have opinions. It takes more than opinions to build a Gothic cathedral." Our sacred architecture is an effort to give concrete form to the faith we feel and wish to express. Another way we give form and expression to faith is in liturgy, the concrete words and actions the Church uses to articulate and celebrate its faith. Horace Allen defines faith as, at heart, "an experience of commitment that is received from a community, nurtured in community, and finally tested there, by word and sacrament."[7] Without liturgy, faith would be little more than a mess of pottage. Liturgy is to faith as the Pledge of Allegiance is to patriotism and the Bill of Rights is to democracy.

Liturgy requires a people. The origin of our word liturgy is the Greek word *leitourgia* which combines the words for work (*érgon*) and people (*laós*). In ancient Greece, a liturgy was a public work, meaning something performed for the benefit of the city or state.[8] By definition, liturgy is "the work of the people," the whole people of God. It's not something one individual does, but an act of the whole body. It is not liturgy if only the priest or pastor and the choir are doing the work for spectators who audit the performance. It might be entertaining, it might be inspirational, but it's not liturgy, and it's not worship. One person can meditate, but it takes two or more to do liturgy or worship.

The Apostle Paul wrote in I Corinthians 12:7: "To each is given the manifestation of the Spirit for the common good." From the context of the passage, it is clear that Paul is talking about what is required for the liturgical life of the community. Each and every member brings a special gift to the liturgical mix, contributing to the worship experience of the whole assembly. It's quite possible that each and every member of a worshiping body of less than one hundred could offer some gift or manifestation of the Spirit for the common good. It's a stretch, if not an impossibility, to imagine that each worshiper in a mega church assembly of thousands has an opportunity to contribute much beyond passive attention and money in the coffer. Liturgy is the work of the whole people for the benefit of God and the rest of God's people, nothing less.

WORSHIP

Worship is the common and inclusive word for the life-affirming occasions (rituals) when the Church gathers in public assembly to express their faith (liturgy) in praise, to hear the Word of God, and to respond to God's love with the gifts of their lives. Churches do many things, but the most common and most important thing a church does is worship. Worship is the source and foundation for everything else the Church is and does. If a church's worship lacks integrity, authenticity, hospitality, vitality, and faithfulness, it's safe to say these things will be lacking in the rest of its life.

The concepts of ritual (that which maintains order, builds community, and leads to transformation) and liturgy (that which gives form and substance to the faith of the whole people) gives clarity to our understanding of worship. But the meaning of the word *worship* itself is illuminating. Our English word worship comes from the Old English secular word *weorthscipe*, which literally means *weorth* (worthy) and *scipe* (ship) and means to give worth or respect to someone.[9] We worship that to which we give honor or worth. Moving from the secular to the sacred realm, to worship God means to value, honor, and praise the One who has created us in the divine image and calls us together.

In *The Big Small Church Book*, I used Jesus' Great Commandment: "You shall love the Lord your God with all your heart, and with all your soul, and with all your mind . . . and . . . You shall love your neighbor as yourself" (Mt. 22:37, 39), as a basis for defining worship. Therefore, I define worship as the ritualized response of the Christian community to God's love with the praises of their hearts, the yearnings of their souls, and the ponderings of their minds, so that the community is able to love each other and all of creation as they love themselves. This definition involves the whole person, as well as the community of faith, gives worth (love) to God, and moves to transformative action.

In *Holy the Firm*, Annie Dillard describes the little church on the island where she lives. Her description provides a poignant transition from our exploration of the meaning of worship to our discussion of worship in congregations with fewer than one hundred worshipers. Her description is reminiscent of many smaller congregations, but of few if any larger ones:

I know only enough of God to want to worship him, by any means ready to hand. . . . There is one church here, so I go to it. . . . On a big Sunday there might be twenty of us there; often I am the only person under sixty, and feel as though I'm on a archaeological tour of Soviet Russia. The members are of mixed denominations; the minister is a Congregationalist, and wears a white shirt. The man knows God. . . . "Good morning!" he says after the first hymn and invocation, startling me witless every time, and we all shout back, "Good morning!"

The churchwomen all bring flowers for the altar; they haul in arrangements as big as hedges, of wayside herbs in season, and flowers in vases the size of tubs, and the altar still looks empty, irredeemably linoleum, and beige. We had a wretched singer once, a guest from a Canadian congregation, a hulking blond girl with chopped hair and big shoulders, who wore tinted spectacles and a long lacy dress, and sang, grinning, to faltering accompaniment, an entirely secular song about mountains. Nothing could have been more apparent than that God loved this girl. . . .

The higher Christian churches—where, if anywhere, I belong—come at God with an unwarranted air of professionalism, with authority and pomp, as though they knew what they were doing, as though people in themselves were an appropriate set of creatures to have dealings with God. I often think of the set pieces of liturgy as certain words which people have successfully addressed to God without their getting killed. In the high churches they saunter through the liturgy like Mohawks along a strand of scaffolding who have long since forgotten their danger. If God were to blast such a service to bits, the congregation would be, I believe, genuinely shocked. But in the low churches you expect it any minute. This is the beginning of wisdom.[10]

In Annie Dillard's experience, size is a critical factor in determining the nature of a worshiping congregation. I believe she's right; but if so, why? Why are numbers so important? How can congregations on the smaller end of the spectrum worship in the most authentic and size appropriate way? How can we insure that what we do in worship, how we do it, and why we do it, fits the number of people present and is the work of the people? How can we apply all of this to our own situation? These questions are the work order for the rest of this book. Pastors, lay leaders, and congregations who pursue these questions with vigilance and creativity will discover new life in their worship and new meaning in their lives.

Questions:

1. How would you define Worship?
2. Identify one of the most memorable and meaningful worship experiences of your life. What made it so?

Suggestion:

Hold a discussion of these questions with one or more groups in your church or in a series of brief moments within your worship service.

TWO

WORSHIP THAT FITS AND WORKS

As we all know, a big mansion is not simply a bungalow with more rooms, a big party is not simply an intimate dinner with more people, a big metropolitan hospital is not simply a clinic with more beds and more doctors, a big corporation is not simply a family firm with more employees and products, a big government is not simply a town council with more branches.[1]

Kirkpatrick Sale believes that size is the fundamental difference in the nature of social organizations. A conversation I had at the University of Mississippi in the mid-1980s revealed to me how right Sale is. I was invited to the university to present three lectures on small churches, rural churches, and small church ministry to a regional gathering of Southern Baptist officials. After the third lecture, an area minister who worked with little conservative churches, "as far back in the sticks of Alabama as you can go," engaged me in conversation. He felt my presentations were very interesting and on target because the way I described small churches was "precisely like the small churches [he] worked with." This was an eye-opener for me because, up to that point, most of my experience had been with moderate-to-liberal, New England, United Church of Christ churches—churches few would imagine bear much similarity to rural, southern, conservative Southern Baptist churches.

I realized then, as never before, that size is more important than theology, cultural or ethnic identity, denominational affiliation, or location in determining the nature and behavior of a congregation. Let me say that again. **Size is the most important variable in determining the nature of any congregation.** This conclusion has been confirmed through my work with such diverse groups as: United Church of Christ churches from Maine to Hawaii, and Washington to Texas; Weslyan Methodists in Canada; the Reorganized Church of Later Day Saints and Southern Baptists in the Midwest; Episcopalians in California; Methodists in Tennessee; Lutherans in Missouri; and Presbyterians in Ohio and southern Georgia.

Why is this so? Primarily, it is because of the dynamics of social organization and levels of relationship. A small organization requires only a simple organizational structure. The larger it grows, the more complex it becomes. Communication becomes more difficult. Procedures become bureaucratic. It takes longer to make decisions, and, then, to act upon them. People have little awareness of the work as a whole and feel less invested in it. A neighborhood medical clinic is a community organization. A university teaching hospital is a vast institution. Both have medical care in common, but it's difficult to recognize them as belonging to the same field of endeavor. The number and nature of relationships make all the difference in how it feels and functions.

RELATIONSHIPS DEFINE THE CHURCH

In any organization, there are multiple levels of relationship—intimate, genuine, functional, superficial, and nonexistent. The way an organization feels and functions is determined by the number and depth of relationships that are present when it is gathered. This mathematical formula identifies the number of relationships in any group, which then will determine how it will function:

Number of Relationships = $\dfrac{\text{Number2} - \text{Number}}{2}$

Here's how it works. Let's say you had a terrible snow storm at Maple Avenue Methodist Church and only four people arrived at church. You wanted to know how many relationships were present among those four. Multiply the number by itself or square it: 4 x 4 = 16. From that answer, subtract the original number: 16 − 4 = 12. Divide that answer by 2 and you discover that among the four people there were six relationships. If that doesn't sound right, test it. Draw a square and number each corner, 1, 2, 3, 4, representing your four worshipers. Draw lines between each of the four persons, indicating a relationship. There's a relationship between 1 and 2, between 2 and 3, between 3 and 4, between 4 and 1, between 1 and 3, and between 2 and 4, for a total of 6 intimate relationships. This intimately shared storm experience could very well cement and color their relationships well into the future.

The next Sunday the usual 20 people showed up. Do the math:

20 x 20 = 400 − 20 = 380 ÷ 2 = 190 genuine relationships

These 20 have gone through thick and thin together, and, while they may have squabbled occasionally, they have been like family to one another.

The next Sunday the church pillar's grandchild was baptized and 40 attended.

40 x 40 = 1600 − 40 =1560 ÷ 2 = 780 functional relationships

These 40 liked what they saw, kept coming back, and soon they all, or almost all, knew and cared about one another.

The Christmas Eve service came and all 40 brought relatives or friends to experience the church they were so excited about and 80 attended.

80 x 80 = 6400 – 80 = 6320 ÷ 2 = 3160 mostly secondary relationships
All 80 were highly impressed and wanted to be part of such a successful church, so they all started attending more or less regularly, joined the church, and got actively involved. Quite possibly, by the following Christmas, most were involved in a congenial working relationship with one another, but most didn't know too many people very well.

Another Christmas Eve service came around and each of the 80 brought two visitors to the service (held in the high school auditorium while a new, larger sanctuary was being built).

240 x 240 = 57,600 – 240 = 57,360 ÷ 2 = 28,680 mostly superficial or nonexistent relationships
Only about half the visitors eventually connected and committed. Attendance plateaued at about 175, and there was room to spare in the new sanctuary.

The church of twenty had a special and solid intimacy. On most Sundays, most were present. If someone was missing, that person was called to make sure he or she was all right. If someone got a better job, the whole church celebrated. If someone's mother died, they all grieved. Almost everyone had some responsibility in making sure the Sunday experience came off as it was supposed to. Worship didn't begin until they were through greeting and catching up with one another. They shared joys and concerns, but the sharing was more ritual than information sharing because everyone already knew and cared about the pain and pleasure that touched the lives of each other. While the quality of singing might not have been great, they sounded more like thirty when they were singing a favorite hymn. The preacher had to be careful what she preached because the listeners knew if she was talking specifically about them, and they knew when she was not talking her walk. Even if the offering plate wasn't full, there was always just enough money to meet the needs of the church and its people.

This church of twenty felt quite different when it became a church of forty. With forty, there was a sense of well-being and optimism as the pews were filled, and there was more money in the offering plates. Most of the original twenty noticed there was a little less intimacy and more order. Some felt a little less needed and slept in more often. The shyer and newer folks were a little more reluctant about sharing their joys and concerns and probably didn't know all the others by name. With a reduced feeling of intimacy, the preacher was a little more formal in language and delivery.

The church felt and behaved somewhat differently when it became a church of eighty. The choir was bigger and sang more complex and formal music. Those who tried out were channeled into ushering or spectating if they couldn't carry a tune or harmonize. It seemed as though fewer people participated in hymn singing. The preacher's sermons were more impersonal and a tad more polished. People were less tolerant of children in worship (especially the children of newer folks) because of the increased noise more children make. Rather than coming early and staying late to visit, many started arriving at or just after the beginning of worship and leaving right afterwards. Visitors slipped in and out unnoticed. The attendance and offering were not four times larger than they were when it was a church of twenty. Most were aware that there were people present they didn't know, at least not well.

When the church leveled off at about 175, things were radically different. Two worship services had been tried, but the results were disappointing. Old-timers were complaining that new folks were taking over. Attendees segregated themselves by age, tenure, and interest. Some were realizing that they weren't talking to as many folks as they used to and that worship was becoming an individualized, private experience. The hiring of two staff members resulted in less lay leadership in worship. The pastors did most of the leading while the worshipers listened more and participated less. The decision to alternate preaching resulted in confusion about the church's theology, vision, and mission. Worship felt more rehearsed and formal. More and more complained they couldn't see or hear very well as the distance between pulpit and spectators seemed lengthened. People were judging worship more by its polish than by its poignancy. Their sharing of joys and concerns had become a perfunctory listing of names of those for whom they would pray. Few prayers were offered since most of those people weren't known to most of the attendees. Maple Avenue Methodist Church carried the same name, but that was about all that was the same.

WHAT IS A SMALL CHURCH?

In presentations about small churches, the most frequently asked question is: How do you define a small church? I prefer to answer that a church is small when it fulfills the twenty-seven characteristics of a small church listed in the preface of this book. Some have defined small churches by what they supposedly can't do, such as paying full-time salaries, offering full-service programs, maintaining full-service buildings, or having enough volunteers to staff traditional church organizations. Others have determined a church is small when compared to bigger churches surrounding it or to its former size. But people persist in wanting a number that separates small from not small. Since the label small is not a complimentary label in our culture, most questioners hope they have enough people to place them in a category larger than small.

About twenty years ago, the accepted criteria for a small church was two hundred members or less. Lyle Schaller, and others, recognized that this was a pretty nebulous distinction. First, a church of two hundred can be very different from a church of fifty. Second, some churches of two hundred are able to keep almost all of their people active while others may list two hundred on the rolls, but have only forty in the pews.

So Schaller offered a better way of measuring church size.[2] He used worship attendance to determine seven categories of churches and gave them the following descriptive names and nicknames.

- The church of up to 40 in worship is a *Fellowship Church* and is called a "Cat" church because it has several cat-like qualities (such as independence and tenaciousness).
- A *Small Church* has 40 to 100 in worship and is called a "Collie" church because it's loyal, wants to be loved, and may nip at visitors.
- The *Middle-Sized Church* averages between 100 and 175 and is nicknamed a "Garden" because a garden has much variety, and a gardener's work is never done.
- A church with 175 to 225 is an *Awkward Church* and is called "The House," since a house requires many specialized skills to handle all the responsibilities.
- The *Large Church* attracts 225 to 450 and is known as "The Mansion," because it requires an enormous amount of help to keep it kept up.
- A church of 450 to 700 is a *Huge Church* or a "Ranch" and depends primarily on hired hands.
- A church of more than that is a *Mini-Denomination* or a "Nation" and has all the clout and problems of any large nation.

WORSHIP WITH FEWER THAN ONE HUNDERED

The focus of this book is worship in Fellowship and Small Churches, churches with fewer than one hundred in worship. Because two categories are combined, differences can be expected even among churches with fewer than one hundred. These are the churches I know best, understand, and for whom I have a particular affinity. This is a size that has been almost entirely ignored in the literature about worship. For example, in my rather extensive library about small churches, there are only two thin books about worship in smaller churches: one written ten years ago and one twenty years ago. Other worship books give little if any attention to the dynamics of size in worship. For the most part, seminary teaching in worship and liturgy is done by those who've been successful in, studied about, or are entranced by larger churches. The general assumption seems to be that the number of worshipers is largely irrelevant to the nature, conduct, and purpose of worship. On the other hand, I believe those who learn how to conduct worship for three hundred probably won't have a clue about worshiping with thirty.

There are three important reasons why this book focuses on worship in churches with fewer than one hundred present:

- **At least two-thirds of all Protestant churches have worshiping congregations of less than one hundred,** and most probably will not grow much beyond that.
- As has already been noted, their worship is going to be very different from larger churches, simply because of the dynamics of numbers. They will not be able to get the help they need from most of the generic literature and seminary education.
- Most importantly, I'm concentrating on the smaller worship experience because this worship has the potential to be the work of *all* the people, and congregations of this size have the potential to more fully be a Christian community that makes a larger difference in the lives of their people.

In the late 1980s, the United Church of Christ researched the correlation between church membership and worship attendance. The results were startling, but were ignored. The results showed that a church of fifty members or less averaged 84 percent of their membership in worship each Sunday, while churches of more than one thousand averaged 30 percent of their membership in worship. This brings up two intriguing questions.

First, why do denominations put most of their evangelism dollars in growing and resourcing larger churches, when the result appears to be an increase in apathetic church members? Second, what is it about the larger worship and church experience that results in, or can't prevent, an apathetic response? Would it be more faithful and effective to grow more smaller churches of more dedicated worshipers than larger churches of less dedicated worshipers? I believe it would be prudent to study the efficacious characteristics of worship in smaller churches to determine how these characteristics might be replicated or adapted to assist larger congregations feel and act smaller despite their larger size. This book could be a helpful resource for larger churches.

There's a conundrum at work here. Worship in smaller numbers seems to better fulfill the essence of Christian worship (being the work of all the people and building Christian community), while the Christian faith mandates evangelism (being an inviting, including, and good news-sharing people). It might appear that my affirmation of smaller churches ignores the importance of evangelism. Not true. Using the principles and practices described in this book, the churches I've pastored have all reversed decades of decline and grown both larger and more faithful. In each place, we've utilized strategies that have maintained the positive qualities of smallness while additional people were attracted to and assimilated into our community of faith.

The church I currently serve in San Rafael is very much aware of numbers. We have just rebuilt our sanctuary and made it slightly smaller, more intimate, and more inclusive, even while the church grows. Our new sanctuary, which can seat up to one hundred twenty, facilitates a liturgy that is the work of all the people and promotes a communal rather than individual experience. Our understanding of worship emphasizes the communal participation of all the people. We feel worship of less than one hundred can be qualitatively more effective than worship with more than one hundred. We've accepted the possibility that, at some point, we may need to start a second worship service or even a second congregation as part of the First Congregational Church of San Rafael. We will remain a small church even as we are evangelical and grow.

The essential first step in leading worship when there is not a crowd is helping those present believe they're not fools or failures, but the right size to participate in this vital endeavor. Without a doubt, the most serious problem plaguing smaller church is weak self-esteem and low morale. Whether we're talking pumpkins, muscles, salaries, or skyscrapers, we live in a society that worships bigness. I've used the word sizeism to describe this fixation. Our language reveals this bias. Typical synonyms for big are: great, considerable, substantial, generous, ample, comprehensive, imposing, tremendous, stupendous, mighty, heroic, and full-grown. Typical synonyms for small are: runt, shrimp, small fry, poky, piddling, dinky, one-horse, pint-sized, undersized, limited, narrow-minded, meager, unimportant, niggardly, petty, and puny. Seeing how our vocabulary illustrates our culture's bias for big over small, most small churches would rather be larger. We need to continually work at reversing or preventing any size-related inferiority complex.

We need to help people see that worshiping more effectively is not the same thing as filling the pews. Help people discern that being faithful is not synonymous with being successful. Demonstrate the advantages inherent in worshiping with fewer than one hundred. Make sure everything that's done in worship fits the number present. Don't do anything that needs more people than you have. Preach the remnant theology of the Old Testament. Sing "O for a Hundred Tongues to Sing." Remind people that while five thousand were fed, Jesus reserved the Lord's Supper for the twelve apostles. Help them rediscover that the first churches were house churches and that almost all churches had fewer than one hundred in worship until the latter half of the twentieth century. Capitalize on the twelve principles and fifteen practices that follow.

CHALLENGES FOR SMALLER CONGREGATIONS

There may well be problems and handicaps to be surmounted when you're worshiping with less than one hundred. Your church may not be able to afford its own full-time, ordained pastor. You are not alone. At least one-third of Protestant churches have pastors who aren't full-time. I have been bivocational and relied on supplementary income most of my ministry—and loved it. Many churches share a pastor with another church. This requires cooperation and juggling, but it can be done. Many churches do very well with committed and gifted lay pastors. The principles and practices that follow depend more on creativity, sensitivity, and conscientiousness than on conventional approaches to church and ministry.

Many smaller congregations cope with facility difficulties. Some may be small churches worshiping in cavernous spaces built for once-large congregations. Architects have been called upon to make these spaces more fitting. Chapels or meeting rooms have provided a more conducive worship environment while the rest of a building was rented out or shared with a nonprofit organization. Church buildings have been recycled (sold) while the church downsized into a living room, storefront, or neighboring church. The church I served for fourteen years had previously lost its traditional New England church building in a failed church merger and found new life in an old colonial house. The Metcalf Memorial Chapel was very economical and communal while it served us and the community extremely well.

These alternatives should be viewed not as stumbling blocks or defeats, but as strategic and creative opportunities. Rather than hanging on to shrines to what they once were, many smaller churches have chosen to timeshare with other smaller churches by sharing one facility that meets all their needs, provides opportunity for cooperation, and symbolizes good stewardship.

Small worshiping communities often are confronted by other challenges. Perhaps your church cannot afford someone to be your preacher/worship leader. If you are a lay person who has chosen to read this book, it may be that *you* have spiritual gifts for worship leadership. If not you, someone in your little flock may. Don't have someone who can preach? The Word of God can be heard just as well in a well-planned twenty to thirty minute Bible study as through a sermon.

Perhaps there aren't enough singers for a choir with four part harmony. Choirs can strengthen worship, but they aren't essential. The only biblical requirements for Christian worship are hearing the Word, praying, and sharing the sacrament. Perhaps there is no one to play the organ. Then use a piano as we do in San Rafael. Perhaps there's no one to play the piano. Is there some-one who can lead unaccompanied singing? If you have or can find someone skilled in computer technology, it's not difficult or expensive to have your congregation's favorite music accompanied by computer/CD ROM technol-ogy. I know a church that did and liked its computer-assisted music better than what it once had.

Your church may be experiencing other impediments to the kind of worship you desire. If the goal is not polished worship like the larger churches may have, but worship that praises God, stretches the mind, feeds the soul, and refreshes the spirit in ways that fit your people and your numbers, you can faithfully and effec-tively compensate for any limitation you're encountering.

Questions:

1. Do you agree that size is the most important variable in determining the nature of a church? Why or why not?
2. Use the mathematical formula and discover how many real or unreal-ized relationships were present in your sanctuary last Sunday? How would your church be different if there were half as many present? Twice as many?
3. Does your church feel and act like the nickname Schaller gives churches of your size? How? Why?
4. How does your church's self-esteem and morale help or hinder the quality of your worship?

Suggestion:

Gather some people, discuss the ideas of this chapter, and then name and dis-cuss any perceived impediments to optimum worship for your particular church. Without worrying about practicality, brainstorm as many conceivable responses as you can. Identify one or two with which you might want to experiment. Try implementing one or both.

THREE

TWELVE PRINCIPLES FOR UNDERSTANDING WORSHIP WITH FEWER THAN ONE HUNDRED

assume that you are reading this book because you care about God's Church, or because you have some involvement with or curiosity about smaller congregations. I assume that you, like me, don't already have all the answers. I've examined everything I've learned about worship with smaller churches from my own experience and from that of others. Desiring to be helpful to God's smaller churches and to you, I've collected these learnings, given them structure, and distilled them into twelve principles that provide a basic understanding of the nature of worship when there are fewer than one hundred worshipers and fifteen practices which build upon the twelve principles.

Some of what follows is simple common sense. Other ideas may sound somewhere between unconventional and heretical. Reconsider your assumptions, as well as mine, then make your own judgment. All that follows is based on two fundamental convictions. The first is that communities of faith, ranging from two to one hundred (the arbitrary limit I'm using here), can worship in ways fully pleasing to God and fully edifying for those engaged in liturgical activity. The second conviction is that if these congregations wish to fully please God and fully realize the potential of their worship experience, they must customize their worship in ways that fit their numbers as well as their other defining characteristics.

I encourage both you and your people to carefully consider these ideas, think about them both playfully and prayerfully, and then creatively respond to them. They are not the last word about worship with smaller numbers, but I hope they are a fresh word, maybe even a new word. The twelve principles are concepts that need to be understood before you begin constructing worship for less than one hundred. The fifteen practices that follow are building blocks for constructing your church's worship experience.

PRINCIPLE # 1: Worship Is about the Worthiness of God and Ourselves

If you want to build a ship, don't drum up people together to
collect wood and don't assign them tasks and work, but rather
teach them to long for the endless immensity of the sea.
—Antoine de Saint-Exupery

We come to worship not because we always have, or think we ought to, or have
nothing better to do, or because they pay us to plan it and do it. According to
the word *worship*, we come to worship in order to give worth to God and
because it has worth or value for us.

It's easy to be discouraged when not many attend worship, and easy to take
the few who do for granted. Would you work harder to plan worship for the
large regional meeting of your denomination? Would you spend more time on
the sermon if the President of the United States were going to attend this
Sunday? We probably all would, but let us not forget that it is Holy God, Jesus
Christ, and the ever present Spirit for whom we design worship. And let us not
forget that God loves the retarded child, and the two or three, at least as much
as God loves the President of the United States or the vast crowd. These all
deserve our very, very best.

Remember the old story about the substitute preacher who arrived on a
snowy morning and discovered that only the old deacon-farmer had been able
to get there? The preacher asked whether they should cancel worship. The
deacon-farmer drawled, "Well, if only one cow comes in from the field to be
fed and milked, I feed and milk her." Seeing the logic in that, the preacher
proceeded to conduct the whole worship service, including singing a solo,
preaching a forty-five minute sermon, praying at length, and taking the offering. Over an hour and a quarter later, he asked the deacon-farmer, "How was
that?" The deacon-farmer gave the question careful thought and answered:
"Well, if only one cow comes in from the field, I don't feed her all the hay in
the hayloft!" This corny story reminds us that even one cow deserves to be fed,
but that it's important to tailor the feeding to the number eating.

Whenever I'm disappointed by the attendance at any gathering, I quote
Jesus to myself: "For where two or three are gathered in my name, I am there
among them" (Mt. 18:20). If God discerns our disappointment, God will know
we are unfaithful. If the people perceive our disappointment, they will likely
feel that we are disappointed in them and that the occasion is probably not
worthy of their attendance either. For worship to work, both we and our people
need to believe that there is no more important thing for us to be doing right
then, whether nine or ninety-nine are present.

Our church in San Rafael is fourteen miles from the Golden Gate Bridge and San Francisco, one of the most fascinating cities in the world. It's also in the middle of some of the most beautiful geography anywhere. When and if people here can get themselves out of bed on a Sunday morning, there is an endless array of great and tempting things to do within fifty miles. Yet most of our busy people are present almost every Sunday. I frequently am tempted to wonder why. Their attendance and their words tell me that giving worth to God, finding worth in their own lives, and sharing in the community that is our church are more valuable to them than staying home or indulging in all those other beckoning temptations.

Before starting this book, I surveyed our congregation's feelings about our worship. Here are some of their responses when asked why they get out of bed and come to church:

- (From a visitor) "I will choose to come back because of the singing and how emotionally and spiritually moved I am."
- "It's my family. The people are friendly, interesting, warm, and concerned, and not too 'churchy.'"
- "How can you go wrong with this quiet time with God and friends?"
- "This community loves each other and puts that love into action through service. I am nurtured, taught, and given opportunities to serve."
- "Coming together as a very diverse congregation is enriching, and I deeply appreciate your most thoughtful order of worship, choice of hymns, and sermon preparation. Each Sunday experience serves to stretch me."
- "I love the warm people; the chance to be quiet and introspective; and the mental and spiritual stimulation; and the reverent atmosphere without being stuffy."

I have a hunch the people in your pews attend for similar reasons.

One thing that has been accomplished in San Rafael has been to increase the belief that worship is a priority in our lives. This has been accomplished by communicating that worship is not an irrelevant activity, but rather a serious matter, by providing a worship service that is well-planned, including a customized, attractive bulletin; by having a worship experience that is fresh and relevant to the lives of these particular people; by seeking to make our worship space more conducive to worship; and by worshiping in ways that make our people feel like essential participants rather than nonessential spectators.

Look again at the quotation by Antoine de Saint-Exupery at the beginning of this section. When worship has genuine worth, it is more than an event to attend or a task to do. Rather, worship that has worth or is awe-inspiring will spark the imagination, sharpen the vision, communicate truth, kindle passion, and motivate people to get on with being faithful.

Phillips Brooks, famous pastor at Trinity Church in Boston, was teaching a seminary preaching course. He broke into one student's dispirited sermon and inquired, "Do you expect to change every person in your congregation every time you preach?" The student stammered, "Well, not every one every time." Brooks thundered back, "That's your problem!" Worship is about giving worth to God and finding worth in ourselves so that we can build worth in our world. No congregation has too few people to make that an unworthy task.

Question:

1. Why do you think the people in your congregation get out of bed and come to worship at your church?
2. If you are the pastor, would you get out of bed to come to your church? Why or why not?

Suggestions:

1. Ask your congregation to write down why they come to worship; record the responses, post the list, and then ask them to continue adding to it. Publish the list in your newsletter or bulletin.
2. Ask your congregation to list how their worship could give more worth to God and have more worth for themselves. What changes would be necessary?

PRINCIPLE #2: Worship Is the Most Important Thing Smaller Churches Do

The raison d'etre for most small churches is
the Sunday morning worship service.[1]

It seems a wonder to me that in our dull little
town we can gather together to sing some great hymns,
reflect on our lives, hear some astonishing scriptures
(and maybe a boring sermon; you take your chances),
offer some prayers and receive a blessing.[2]

Larger churches are noted for many things—a multi-faceted educational ministry, a variety of small group opportunities, a seven-day-a-week program, a beautiful and functional building, more than one minister, and a music ministry.

Smaller churches have difficulty measuring up in these areas. But there are areas in which they can excel and stake a claim. One is in taking care of one another. Another is worship.

Worship is the one most important thing all small churches do. Why? The answer is found in the I Corinthians 13 trinity of faith, hope, and love. Most smaller churches are found in rural or small town America, in inner cities, or among ethnic and immigrant groups. Life is not easy for many people in these settings. I spent many years pastoring in rural America where farmers struggle to keep farming, where young people flee to the educational and employment opportunities of more populated areas, and where rural values often seem out of step with a faster paced culture. Urban smaller churches often feel dwarfed and intimidated by the size, swirl, and pressures of life around them. Almost a quarter of the congregations in our regional United Church of Christ conference in Northern California are ethnic churches—Samoan, Phillipino, Chinese, African American. All but a couple of these are smaller churches. Many of the people of these churches depend on their church to be an island of identity, stability, and security in a society that is too often dismissive or hostile.

When smaller churches gather to worship, their faith in God and God's gracious love is strengthened. They feel more hopeful as the ties that bind them in Christian community are strengthened. In the experience of worship and community, they experience God's love and the love of each other. In biblical times, the community of faith was most faithful when it was a remnant community. Many of these churches are remnant communities in our time. For their people, the church is much more than a voluntary association, and their worship more than an optional activity. Their church and its worship is the touchstone that gives them identity, meaning, and purpose.

There are additional vital reasons why worship is the most important activity of smaller churches. Larger churches have multiple programmatic doorways. In smaller churches, the door into worship is the primary doorway into their congregations. Because the people of our church remember that a first visit into a strange environment is a daunting experience, our church is ready to lessen their anxiety. Friendly greeters are at the door. Visitors are offered literature about our church. We give a pen with our name and address as a symbolic welcoming present. Visitors are introduced to others. Children are also greeted. Visitors are invited to sign our guest book with name and address, so I can write them a welcoming letter that invites them back and offers pastoral services. Our board of ministry is urged to make sure no one sits alone. We try to have an atmosphere of hospitality that treats every visitor as a special guest. Most importantly, we try to provide these guests with a fresh and hopeful worship experience that makes them want to return. Rather than planting myself in one spot after worship, I approach visitors on their way out, encourage them to stay for refreshments, and introduce them to someone else with whom they might connect. Every church needs to carefully consider whether their visitors experience a cold shoulder or warm hospitality.

Intimacy, immediacy, and involvement are the most important characteristics of smaller church worship. In such a setting people are more likely to have their lives touched and their needs addressed rather than when they are merely a face in the crowd. We take the concept of *sanctuary* seriously. In our worship time and space, people are safe and free to be themselves, to open their lives to their God, to await a transforming moment of grace. It's not uncommon for a first-timer to share a joy or concern or to request prayer. Our bulletin says that we are an open and affirming congregation welcoming all God's people into our shared life. We have made our renovated facility physically accessible. We're now working to make ourselves just as accessible.

One thing smaller churches can offer that is much more difficult in larger churches is *community*: a place where and people with whom persons can connect, contribute, and belong. Community is probably the greatest unmet desire of people in our culture. More than anything else, smaller churches and their worship are the right size to provide that. The San Rafael church is very intentional about community. The vocabulary of our liturgy is plural (we and our). Most Sundays we have a few minutes of greeting at the beginning of our liturgy when people move about, greet one another, and welcome newcomers. In our worship survey, our joys and concerns time was the second highest-rated component of our worship. Visitors often find themselves opening up to people who were strangers only a few moments before. Our low drop-out rate is evidence of our relatively high level of community.

Without a worship experience that is real and redeeming, a smaller church will not have the courage to carry on, and perhaps it should not. If it does have that kind of experience, it will bear any hardship and pay any price to carry on. Everything else that is part of the life of a smaller church begins in worship: the caring, educational, outreach ministries and the organizational tasks of the church. We pastors resent the tired joke that we only work one hour a week. In fact, the hours on Sunday morning, from the time I drive into the parking lot until I leave, are the most satisfying, productive, and exhausting hours of my week. If I have not worked well then, I will not be able to make up for it later.

Question:

Do you agree or disagree that worship is the most important thing a small church does? Why or why not?

Suggestions:

1. With whichever group(s) you meet this week, ask them to list all the important things that happened the last time you gathered for worship. Be specific, share the stories, name the names.
2. Ask members to help you discover how the time your church comes together could be even more important for the people of your church.

PRINCIPLE #3: Smaller Churches Can Worship Very Well

We make an enormous mistake if we don't tailor our worship to enhance the distinctive qualities of small churches. We should make sure our worship is characterized by what small churches do best.[3]

One of my greatest delights and frustrations is attending denominational, regional, and national gatherings or ecumenical events. There is great effort to produce what I call pomp and circumstance worship at each. The finest wordsmiths craft a ponderous liturgy. As many officials and representatives of different ethnic and interest groups as possible are assigned bits of the service to lead. Many use their time at the microphone as if it is their last God-given opportunity to enlighten the world. Various languages are used. There's lots of singing; but, unfortunately, often the music is new and difficult to sing. Seldom do those attending get to hear a chorus of hundreds sing old favorites. A great preacher (great because he or she is imported from somewhere else and has a pedigree) preaches far longer than listeners can concentrate. The logistics of serving communion to several hundred worshipers in less than half an hour makes one realize that the miracle of feeding five thousand was not that Jesus provided enough food, but that he got everyone fed before anyone starved. Throw in visual effects, liturgical dancers, and massive choirs and you have quite a show—one that usually lasts much too long.

These mass worship events are impressive and memorable, but seldom do I experience them as engaging worship. They are more performance than genuine involvement. Their implied message for pastors and lay folk from local churches is that this is what real worship is, this is what we should aspire to when we return home. When and how will we learn that a memorable, maybe inspiring event is not necessarily worship? Maybe this is why Jesus avoided the temple through his whole ministry and stayed among the villages, in the synagogues, and by the lake shore. To copy mass worship experiences in our smaller settings is both foolish and futile. It would be wiser to concentrate on doing well the worship that fits our size and context.

The principle here is that smaller churches can worship very well, but must do so in ways that are authentic, indigenous, and size-appropriate. If worship is to be authentic, it must be compatible with how the Church has understood Christian worship through the ages. It must reflect their best sense of who God is and what God desires of us. And it must honestly reflect who the members of the church are. For them to worship well, they will probably need to worship differently from what many books describe and from how their pastors were trained to lead worship.

Historically, the Church has believed that worship is a communal action that is offered in gratitude as a gift to God, is a receiving of the Word of God and the sacramental gifts of God, and is a responding to the gifts of God with our own gifts. Anything less is not what worship is meant to be. The God who is worshiped is not a god created in our own image or as we want a god to be, but the very finest, most real, and most awesome God we can conceptualize and experience. If our worship is to be authentic and indigenous, it must reflect who we are. It should be in our own way of speaking; it should use the music of our own people and our own soul; and it should utilize imagery, symbolism, and architecture that communicates for us and to us. A people's authentic worship reflects who they are culturally, the times and locale in which they live, and the faith of their hearts and minds. To worship in authentic and indigenous ways is not as easy and predictable as worshiping the way we always have, or lifting it from our denomination's book of worship, but it is a lot more enjoyable, faithful, and effective.

A smaller church will worship well if it does so in ways that fits its numbers. A chamber ensemble will not try to play music written for a full orchestra. A gardener will not try to cultivate an acre garden with a hoe. Our worship is planned for the number anticipated. For example, I don't ask our congregation to learn a new and tricky hymn if our music director or half of our choir is away on vacation. After our children leave for church school, about forty worshipers remain in worship. With this number present, it is more workable to invite the congregation to give their interpretation of the scripture or to finish an open-ended sermon than if there were one hundred forty present. I'm more likely to use names of parishioners in the sermon when the congregation all know one another. I'm more likely to use a piece of video as a sermon illustration when the furthest worshiper is only forty feet from the monitor. These are only a few of the many ways worship can be tailored to the number of worshipers.

Smaller churches enhance their worship when they make it their work to involve as many people as possible. I examined two typical San Rafael worship services and counted the number of times the congregation did something other than listen during each one hour service. These included actions like lighting candles, making announcements, greeting others at the beginning of worship, reading different parts of the liturgy, singing (six or seven times, plus the choir's music), telling the children's story and getting comments from the children, sharing joys and concerns, ushering and contributing, and the passing of the peace. Frequently, people other than the designated worship leaders will participate in the scripture reading and in the sermon time. The number of involvements I counted did not include other kinds of participation like praying, active listening during the sermon, and sharing communion elements. In one service, our people participated twenty times and in the other twenty-two times. There could have been more.

Søren Kierkegaard, nineteenth century theologian, suggested that in genuine worship God is the audience, not the congregation. The congregation are the actors, not the pastor or preacher. The pastor or preacher is the prompter. Similar to that metaphor, I see myself as the director of a play or conductor of an orchestra, not as the lead actor or virtuoso soloist. When I design worship, the longest anyone sits and does nothing but listen is ten to twelve minutes. Perhaps this sounds like chaos or busy work, a disruption of the quiet or solemnity of worship, and, true, there isn't much solemnity, but there is great reverence. Our people are comfortable with participating and acting their roles in the drama of worship with skill, joy, and reverence. As the quality and quantity of participation in worship increases, I find my sermons are getting shorter (ten to twelve minutes), and the words are more carefully crafted, more accurately heard and responded to more thoughtfully. One of the most heart-warming compliments I have ever received was from old Carl Nordstedt in Warwick who was heard to say, after sleeping through years of worship, "Well, at least he keeps us awake."

Let me illustrate how worship can really be the work of the people. Let's say we have fifty-five hypothetical worshipers on a Sunday. Two people bring flowers and decorate the sanctuary. Two are greeters and create a hospitable atmosphere. Two make and serve refreshments. Two children light and extinguish the candles. Two people volunteer announcements. An adult and a youth serve as lay readers. An adult and four children speak up during the ministry with children. A woman and child take the offering. One preaches and two respond to the sermon. Twelve are in the youth-adult choir, ten in the children's choir, and two accompany the music. Four share joys and concerns, one counts the house and turns up the thermostat. A total of fifty-one play an active part in worship, leaving four who are still too new or shy to do or say something publicly. And this doesn't count the congregational greeting, singing, praying, and active listening that involves everyone. This hypothetical congregation is a model for doing what it is the right size to do well.

Another way to worship well as a smaller church is to capitalize on being small enough to be flexible and spontaneous. We've easily moved worship locations, changed worship times, and done very different things with our worship services—sometimes on the spur of the moment. Our small size made these changes possible.

Three times in Warwick stand out. One bitterly cold morning, we arrived at the chapel and discovered that the gas floor furnace (the only heat) was out of gas. We all (maybe thirty people) piled into cars and drove to Ted and Marge's home, where Sunday school was conducted upstairs while adults worshiped in their living room. Another time, the night before Pentecost Sunday, I decided to ask everyone to wear the colors of Pentecost (red and white) to worship the next day. Five people made five calls apiece and every person was colorfully dressed the next morning. It was glorious! And then there was a memorable summer Sunday when Derric and Eric, five-year-old twins, were playing outside during worship. Eric climbed up a ten foot maple stump. Soon afterward, brother Derric pounded on the front door (about ten feet from the pulpit) during my sermon, burst into the room, and announced with outrage, "Eric peed on me!" With no reasonable alternative and no large crowd to pacify, we quickly decided to end worship for that Sunday and move on to our refreshments. It was all right because a church of that size is all family without embarrassment, anger, or confusion. We could spontaneously change our plans. This has also been true in the other three churches I served.

What else can small churches do well in worship? Smaller church worship can be personal. I will always remember the time during joys and concerns in Emmetsburg when Chuck North took his wife Laura by the hand (these were two of our shyer members), led her to the front of the sanctuary, and said to the congregation, "Fifty years ago this week Laura and I were married at the front of this sanctuary. I was so nervous I forgot to kiss my bride. So I'm going to do that now." He did, we cheered, and there wasn't a dry eye or a turned down mouth in the congregation.

Small churches have time to be appropriately personal during sacramental occasions. We designed our remodeled sanctuary in San Rafael to make better room for one of our favorite traditions. When we celebrate the Lord's Supper, the whole congregation comes and receives communion by intinction in a family circle around the Lord's Table, or as we also call it, the Family Table. There's one loaf, one cup, one Body of Christ—the Church. Each person can be called by name when the elements are brought around. When a family member comes who has someone sick at home, I can say, for example, "This is the Bread of Life, for you and Margee." Our communion is truly a common experience, not a private one.

Unless we're baptizing siblings, I only baptize one person at a time and only within the context of worship. We produce a special baptism insert for that person, with the baptism certificate reproduced on the cover, within the larger bulletin. With the permission of the parents, the child is carried throughout the congregation so each person can see and perhaps touch the newest member of the church family. Our baptisms are truly an initiation or adoption into God's and the church's family.

Weddings and funerals or memorial services are wonderful times in smaller churches. Since we don't do very many, we can do each one particularly well. One Sunday morning in the Warwick worship room, we had a wedding feast to celebrate the impending marriage of Steve and Fran. Tables decked in white tablecloths replaced pews, and the feast was a potluck meal. At both weddings and funerals, people can be invited to share oral blessings or memories, making the event far more memorable. When we had a memorial service for five-year-old Brian during the Christmas season, we placed his favorite toys under the church Christmas tree. When we had a memorial service for seventy-nine year old Henry, we filled our lattice cross with white calla lilies. The personal nature of these observances make them unforgettable.

Because we are small enough to be personal, our people in San Rafael consider our joys and concerns one of the most significant parts of our worship. We are small enough so that I can get a list of everyone's favorite hymns and guarantee that we will sing them all within the calendar year. The smaller the number of people, the more personal and real we can be to each other. The more personal we are with one another, the more intimate our fellowship becomes and the deeper our sense of community will be. The deeper our sense of community, the more people feel supported and sustained through both the hard and the not so hard times.

To illustrate this last point, it has been documented with careful research that sick people who are prayed for have a higher rate of recovery than those who are not. It's documented that people who are part of supportive relationships and communities and who have something to look forward to live longer than those who do not. In each of the four churches I've known well, the death rate among older active participants was lower than one would expect for the size of our membership and the number of elderly people.[4] Could it be that the number of people who have recovered from serious illness and continued to live meaningful lives was partly because their faith community gave them a reason to live and they felt loved and needed?

Question:

Every church does at least one thing well in worship. What does your particular church do particularly well? Is that size related? What else could it be particularly good at?

Suggestion:

Gather some people, perhaps even in place of your traditional sermon on a summer Sunday, and tell stories of the things that have happened over the years in your church's worship that illustrate and celebrate how a smaller church can worship very well. Have them tell the story of the time they were particularly touched or the time something really important happened. Have one or two primed in advance to get the ball rolling. Someone might be willing to write these up as a piece of your church's history.

PRINCIPLE #4: Smaller Churches Are More Likely to Experience God as Immanent than as Transcendent (and They May Prefer Jesus and the Holy Spirit)

> It is impossible to take the little finger of liturgy without grasping the whole fist of theology.
> —Gerandus van der Leeuw,
> Dutch Reformed liturgical theologian

Theology has been simply defined as God talk, but it's a little more involved to understand theology as talking about the experience of God. Every church has a prevailing, experiential theology, though most members cannot name or articulate it. A church's or a people's theology grows out of its context and particular experience of God. For example, Native Americans, who have lived close to the earth, have experienced God as a part of the very fabric of nature. Latin American indigenous peoples, who have been repressed and subjugated for centuries, experience God as a liberating God who sides with the underclass. Their primary theological model is Our Lady of Guadalupe, who intentionally appeared to a peasant farmer rather than someone from the dominant class. Out of God's limitless range and diversity, God chooses to come to us and is known to us through the time, culture, and locale in which we live.

So it makes sense that those who worship God in a great cathedral will most likely understand and experience God in individual, vertical, and transcendent terms, while those who worship God as part of an intimate community in a smaller church are more likely to understand and experience God in personal, immanent, and communal ways. Size is a fundamental factor in helping shape the theology of a church. The God who is revealed and experienced in many different ways is likely to be understood in particular ways in particular churches.

This important understanding is often overlooked. Pastors arrive at a church and start preaching a theology developed out of a lifetime of experience somewhere else, or after studying Systematic Theology 301 in seminary, or after reading a good book on feminist theology. The people in the pews, who are not at all ignorant, may find such theological posturing more difficult to comprehend and translate than if the preaching was done in classical Greek. When it comes to hymn singing, some clergy may choose to sing "Immortal, Invisible, God Only Wise," while the congregation would rather sing "For the Beauty of the Earth" or "What a Friend We Have in Jesus."

When it comes to praying the pastoral prayer, are we praying to the same aspect of the Trinity as our people, or do we pray to God while they pray to Jesus or the Holy Spirit? When we baptize and administer communion, do we do it out of a classical theological understanding, or do we baptize as an initiation and adoption ritual into the family of God in this place, as well as all times and places? When we quote Jesus at the communion table to "do this in remembrance of me," are they being asked to remember Jesus in a figurative sense or are they invited to remember their own experiences with Jesus? The personal responses are likely to resonate with folks in smaller churches.

The newly arrived, wise, and sensitive pastor will make it a priority to listen to how a representative sampling of a new congregation experience, understand, and talk about their God. Carl Dudley suggests doing this listening in the sanctuary in the person's favorite pew. You cannot be their pastor, spiritual leader, or even friend until they know that you understand not only them, but their God. When you do, you will probably have a life-sustaining and life-transforming ministry among these particular people. If you don't, you probably won't. You can't have a worship life in a church that is the work of the people unless it is conducted in a language they know, is addressed to the God who has brought them this far, and invites them into relationship with the God who is already at work and at home among them.

Here are some clues about the God most likely to be present in a smaller congregation. The people's God will be a personal God who is nearby, available, and approachable. They are likely to experience God as much through their relationships with each other as through private prayer time. For example, when I'm deeply touched, my eyes fill with tears. That happens much more often in an intimate conversation with someone I care about than when praying to a transcendent and distant God. That says to me that I experience and know God interpersonally and immanently more than I do individually and transcendently. A smaller church's God is likely to be a practical or pragmatic God. The people probably have much less interest in hearing speculative preaching about an ethereal God than they do in hearing the preacher talk to them in all honesty about her or his personal relationship with God. Their God is probably more experienced in prayer than in wordy liturgy or impersonal preaching. Their God will be a God involved in their personal and shared history more than a God somewhere out there or contained in New Age spiritualism. Rural people will worship a God found and experienced in nature who really does care if it is raining too much or not enough.

So what does the preacher preach in a church where God is experienced more immanently and interpersonally? Remember that the finest thing Annie Dillard could say about the Congregational pastor in the little island church where she worshiped was that "he knew God." That's not a bad place to begin. Preach the God you know in your heart, the one who sustains you in the dark night of your own soul. Preach the God you experience with the people near you. Reread the epistle accounts in the New Testament and preach out of your church's attempt at faithfulness, just as Paul and his followers taught their churches. Since small churches are more story than treatise, preach with real stories from all of your experiences, not with stories from the Reader's Digest. If yours is a small church, it's likely to be a remnant church (smaller than it once was), so preach the remnant theology of the Old Testament, telling the folks how faith communities have always been most faithful when they have been remnant communities. Honor, encourage, reassure, affirm, and love your people. Don't lecture or scold them. God placed these people in your care.

I supervised two seminary interns who were working in our church. One of our most provocative supervisory sessions occurred in response to the question: What is your primary, fundamental sermon? What I meant was that most preachers have one basic sermon that gets preached in many ways. I have forgotten what they said theirs were, but the question helped me realize that my primary, fundamental sermon is *community*. That's what I believe God most wants us as churches to be. It's what a church will be when it's at its most faithful and effective self. Rather than use the term Kingdom of God, I use the term Community of God. This terminology is less magisterial and more what people hunger for in their deepest selves. I think this theological emphasis has helped create four pretty fair faith communities in Warwick, Shrewsbury, Emmetsburg, and San Rafael. So what is your primary, fundamental sermon and does it fit the primary, fundamental need of your congregation?

In *Making the Small Church Effective*, Carl Dudley quotes a prayer of a woman sitting with her pastor after they had reflected about her experience with God in her little church. Let this poignant prayer lead you to identify what you would pray if you were that honest. What do the people you know best pray as they sit in the place where they are most at home? Here is her prayer:

Lord, I'm tired—so very tired. Please Lord, I don't want any advice. I've heard enough of that over the years. I don't want to be told what I must do. I've been told that often enough. [Is she talking about the kind of preaching she's been hearing for years?] Lord, I just want to sit here in quietness and feel your presence. I want to touch you and to know your touch of refreshment and reassurance. Thank you for this sacred little spot where I have heard your voice and felt your healing touch across the years. Thank you for these dear friends who share this pew with me. Together we have walked the tearlined lanes. We know what it is to be lonely. . . . We also know the comfort and strength of one another and the joy of your presence. [Feeling close to her God and those who have stood with her over the years, she is now ready to get to the heart of her prayer.] O God, the child of my womb has become a drunk. . . . Daily I watch her die before my eyes. Where have I failed, O Lord? How can I find the strength to continue? How can I help my dying daughter find herself?

[Feeling heard and fortified, she is ready to sign off and resume her caring and faithful living.] O God, soon I will be going home to be with you and my husband. I am ready, even eager, but until that day help me to be a help to others. Give me strength to live this day and peace to enjoy it. Amen.[5]

This is the prayer of a woman who knows God, who knows that God knows her, who is at home in her church, and who believes that God has a ministry for her.

Questions:

1. How would you describe the theology of your congregation?
2. With which part of the Trinity—God, Jesus, or the Holy Spirit—do they have most affinity? To which part do you mostly pray?
3. What is your primary, fundamental sermon for your people?

Suggestion:

Remembering that Christ (or God or the Holy Spirit) is present when two or three gather in his name, invite two or three long-time members of your church to sit with you in their sanctuary and reflect on their experience of God among their people. Then read the "Lord, I'm tired" prayer and suggest that the three or four of you pray in the same spirit. Without being afraid of silence or needing to trump one another, pray together.

PRINCIPLE #5: Much More than Worship Happens When They Come to Worship

A friend of mine is a juggler. . . . He doesn't juggle spectacular objects. . . . Just balls. He's intent on doing the simplest thing as well as possible. He can juggle eight balls and keeps trying for nine, which would tie the world's record. I can juggle two balls and sometimes three, so I know just enough to know how really spectacular his achievement is.[6]

We all juggle. And smaller churches, as a whole, juggle more than larger ones. Larger churches diversify and delegate. One committee does one thing and another committee does another thing. They gather one time for one thing and another time for another. There's something for everyone. Their menu is tasty and extensive. Smaller churches have one specialty of the house and all get the same entree with different side dishes. Larger churches are three ring circuses, with simultaneous acts going on in each ring. Smaller churches don't have quite as many acts, but the ones they have all happen in one ring, and many of them happen in rapid-fire fashion.

Since worship is one of the things smaller churches do well and since worship is the time when all the people gather, everything tends to get juggled around the edges. It's not neat, pure, or by the book. In fact, it can be down-right messy, occasionally frenetic, and even exhausting. However, if the church has learned to juggle well, the time together will be a combination of wonderful worship, good-natured chaos, fun, creative and dynamic endeavor, and accomplishment. People will go home having not only just worshiped, but having experienced and expressed church in all of its fullness.

In *The Big Small Church Book*, I describe any faithful and effective church as a 3-M company. The three Ms are the three requirements to which a church must attend in order to be a faithful and effective church—*Ministry, Mission,* and *Maintenance.*

The *Ministry* of the church is what the church does in order to equip itself for its Mission. The Ministry of the church is composed of three components— worship and spiritual nurture, education and disciple making, and the care of one another.

The *Mission* of the church is everything the church does beyond its doors in response to God's love, building the Community of God or the world as God intends it to be. This includes both individual discipleship and collective local-to-global action.

The *Maintenance* aspects of the church are all the rest of the things a church must do in order to faithfully and effectively fulfill its Ministry and Mission. The

Maintenance responsibilities in the church include: building and maintaining church self-esteem and morale; money, property, and policies; new members; leadership recruitment and development; organizational order and development; communications; conflict management; planning; and maintaining outside relationships (community and wider church). A church that only attends to its Ministry responsibilities will be like a well-equipped fisherman who never goes fishing. A church that puts all its energy into its Mission will soon be exhausted. And a church that focuses only on its Maintenance tasks will be like a well-tuned car that is always up on blocks.

In smaller churches, all these tasks—one way or another—tend to happen around the edges when the church gathers to worship. Sometimes they happen intentionally by persons designated to take care of particular tasks. Other times they just happen as folks do what they see needs doing. The San Rafael church is particularly accomplished at this. People here are spread across two counties and are unusually busy in their vocational, community, and family lives, so most of what we do happens on Sunday morning—worship, Christian education, adult forums, community building and care giving, ministry with one another, some board and committee meetings, and special events. It is part of my job to see that we don't juggle more balls than we really need to, that no one person is juggling more than is healthy for that person, and that no one is left out. I also try to see that the undesignated tasks (like morale and self-esteem) are worked on in the midst of the rest. And I insure that we remember that worship is the primary and fundamental tie that binds us, and the time when we can let go of the other things we're juggling.

A typical Sunday morning at First Congregational is like a three-act play. The first act begins when I arrive by 7:00 AM to put the finishing touches on the sermon, see that a display has been put up, answer the phone when a caller wants to know when worship begins, talk with our music director, Tom, and greet early arrivals. These early arrivals (sometimes even visitors) are often given tasks to do in preparation for worship. The choir straggles in a half hour early to polish what they've previously practiced. Our greeters for the day, Richard and Denise, are at the door, welcoming everyone in the spirit of genuine hospitality, handing out bulletins and notices, and attending to visitors. Treasurer Bob is in the administrative office taking care of financial details and alerting me to issues of which I need to be aware. Caryl arrives with Lucile, our oldest member, and then joins other church school teachers in getting themselves organized. Caryl is also our moderator, so often we have matters that need discussing. Luise, or one or two others, are setting up for communion or the coffee hour. Another Bob is turning on the sound system and greeting everyone within reach. Kids are running about while their parents cluster in the courtyard. People keep visiting when the pastor and music director wish they would come in and listen to the whole prelude. By invitation, cajoling, and good-natured maneuvering, we get them all into the sanctuary.

The prelude begins the second act. Afterwards, the pastor says, "Good Morning!" and the congregation answers back, "Good Morning!" The pastor and others take too long making too many announcements, but they're all important and are probably worth doing. Then the congregation is invited to stand, move around, and welcome one another to worship. As I greet folks (especially visitors), I watch what else is happening. People are reaching out to visitors and newcomers. Children and adults are talking to each other. People make a beeline for those they haven't seen in awhile. Shy folks wait for others to take the initiative, and they usually do. There is a warm and good-natured clamor. Tom plays some music to encourage folks to return to their places. This can take as long as five minutes. By now we've become more of a community, less an assortment of individuals. As such, we're ready to worship.

During worship, some tasks of the church are accomplished that are not considered part of the liturgical agenda. We try to be as informative as possible so people will know what's going on. We're conscious that Christian education for all ages is happening during the ministry of children, when the background of scripture is described, during the sermon, and throughout worship. The congregation cares for one another through their conversations before and after worship, through the announcements, and through what is shared during our joys and concerns and prayers. If the board of mission is initiating a special mission emphasis, this will likely become a theme for the whole worship service and perhaps a forum or all-church event after worship. The preacher, by the light of scripture, seeks to strengthen the whole life of this community of faith. The way the sacraments of baptism and communion are observed also deepens the life of the community. Worship always ends with a commission that sends our people out into the world carrying out the mission of the church through word and action. As they leave, they are inspired by a stunning new stained glass window of the earth as seen from space, which is their visual call into a world without boundaries. Tom may use a piece of popular music for the postlude to bridge the theme of the morning with life back in the everyday world.

After worship, the third act of the morning begins. Rather than lining up to recess out of the sanctuary, our people tend to clump up, doing whatever they need to do with one another. I look for visitors and people I haven't seen for awhile. Some adults try to beat the children to the refreshment counter. Girl Scouts may be selling cookies. People sign cards for those who are sick. An ad hoc birthday celebration may happen. During our renovation, a third Bob answered questions about the sanctuary renovation. Teachers talk about what happened in church school. Visitors and members connect. People talk to the pastor about the sermon, some aspect of worship, or a matter of church life. Others confer with people about church affairs or personal matters. Someone may recruit others to sign up to walk in the Church World Service Hunger Walk, bring refreshments, or attend a retreat.

What goes on after worship is that people talk with one another so that relationships can grow and the church can be the church. Frequently, a meeting of one of our boards or committees, or with our church school parents, or prospective members is convened. Occasionally, worship is followed by a pot luck meal or an all-church meeting. Someone's in the office counting money, choir robes are put away, used bulletins are picked up, the Sunday flowers or garden produce is given away, and the pastor is concluding a last word with someone. As the members of the Korean church arrive, our people disperse. More than five hours after arriving at church, the pastor leaves for home after a fruitful and exhausting morning of work as conductor of the work of the people (worship) and co-leader and participant in the rest of the Ministry, Mission, and Maintenance of the church.

This eclectic and sometimes frenetic Sunday morning works well for us. I'm sure it describes a typical Sunday morning in many other smaller churches. This high energy, labor intensive, worship centered, something-for-everyone approach to Sunday morning helps account for the high morale, productivity, and spirited worship that characterize this church. As pastoral leader of this kind of Sunday morning, I'm part juggler, priest, pastor and counselor, rabbi, prophet, secretary, cheerleader, chief executive officer, and bemused observer. Our worship informs, inspires, and convenes the rest of our church life. And the rest of our church life gives our worship energy and purpose. People leave knowing they've been part of something alive and important and their lives have been enriched.

Questions:

1. Describe what happens on Sunday morning at your church. Are you surprised by how much happens or discouraged by how little happens?
2. How do you feel about the author's description of a multi-purpose Sunday morning? Intrigued? Repelled? Affirmed?

Suggestion:

Ask someone with a video camera to record your whole congregation at worship. Watch it with some people to see what you can learn about what happens there. Do you see more choreography or chaos?

PRINCIPLE #6: Their Worship Needs to Be Indigenous, More than Heterogeneous, and Not Homogeneous

> The single most common congregational activity is, in fact, the ritual of a weekly worship event. It is in this event that congregations engage in their most dramatic rituals, their most intentional presentation of who they are … worship is an event that is meant to express the unifying vision of the congregation.[7]

Douglas Walrath, retired professor at Bangor Theological Seminary, knows more about smaller churches than almost anyone. In a conversation with me about preparing people for ministry in smaller churches, he advocated placing seminarians in churches for internships and requiring that they say and do nothing but look and listen for twelve weeks. He thought that students wouldn't have anything worth saying until they had listened for that long, and that they wouldn't know what to do until they'd watched how things were done in that place by that people at that time. This is an intriguing proposal. Doug understands that every congregation, especially a smaller one, has its own indigenous culture that has evolved over time, that is worthy of deep respect, and that determines the ethos out of which authentic worship springs. By *indigenous* I mean the distinctive, home-grown way of being a congregation.

In contrast to what Walrath suggests, much teaching and writing about worship presumes that congregations are pretty homogeneous. Each mainline denomination has its own book of worship with services and resources for the services, occasions, and seasons of the church year. These resources are prepared by liturgical scholars who understand the biblical roots of Christian worship and the historical development of liturgical traditions that have passed down through mostly white, European-American history. The denominational producers of these resources presume that the resources will fill the bill for the churches of their denomination.

This one-liturgy-fits-all approach doesn't work. What speaks to and for one congregation might not speak to or for others or for some people within those congregations. In my denomination, most of our worship resources have been prepared by and for white Euro-American, educated, moderate to liberal, suburban and urban, medium-to-large church, middle aged and older people with a solid Christian heritage. But many people are not included in one or more of those categories. These excluded folk are likely to feel somewhere between uncomfortable and alienated in the generic worship styles that are provided for the mainstream.

What speaks to and for white Euro-American middle-class folks like me won't say as much to other economic, ethnic, and cultural groups. The liturgies and music that are comfortable for well educated, verbal people will leave others tongue-tied and self-conscious. The theological understandings and terminologies that communicate to and for moderate and liberal people won't articulate the faith that conservatives and evangelicals have in their hearts. The language that communicates to east and west coast urbanites may sound like a foreign language in the Farm Belt. Whenever we try to address everyone, someone is left out. We may be One in Christ, but the Christian Church is not one homogeneous whole. Worship that is homogeneous will be broad and inclusive, but it is likely to be shallow, rootless, and neglectful of many.

Some church leaders are becoming conscious of these oversights and are seeking to redress them. Our denomination, like many, has a new hymnal. In addition to some old favorites and some fine new hymns from the dominant culture, there are many hymns from many other cultures. Among the worship resources in the back of the hymnal are a few representations from other cultures. Heterogeneous churches like the San Rafael congregation can enjoy using this wider range of music, and people who are not of white European ancestry may feel a little more included.

I have had the privilege of doing considerable travel in Africa and Latin America and involvement in a wide variety of churches in those cultures, ranging from Roman Catholic to conservative Baptist. I've gained profound insights about other approaches to faith and worship from these experiences, for which I am deeply grateful. My sensitivity and appreciation for heterogeneous expressions of our faith has been heightened. Worship that seeks to be heterogeneous will include more of the whole Community of God, but it will not go as deep as it goes wide. It will not express the deepest yearnings and profoundest understandings of peoples living in particular places at particular times.

The only way to achieve that is with indigenous worship in congregations where there are indigenous roots. Smaller churches are more likely to have these deep growing roots. Why is that?

In our mobile and urban society, larger churches tend to be populated by people who've come from somewhere else and by people who expect to go somewhere else sometime soon. They tend to be oases for sojourners without deep roots. The vision of "church" in these larger congregations tends to be more personal fulfillment and congenial association than lasting commitment and genuine community. These churches will be homogeneous or heterogeneous. There will be little indigenous understanding or experience.

Indigenous people are people with deep growing roots, people who know where they come from, who know who they are, and who know what is authentic—at least in their world. A person *from away* asked an old Maine native if he'd lived in Maine his whole life. After weighing the implications of the question, he answered, "Not yet." My first funeral in my first church was for one of Warwick's town fathers who literally died in the bed in which he was born. The old timer who says, "We've never done it that way before" may be commenting more about the sufficiency of their traditional ways than voicing opposition to new ways. People who are indigenous tend to be suspicious of those who are not—and often for good reason. People who are indigenous have an abundant ritual life, one which has been honed throughout generations of practice.

Small churches, in both rural and urban settings, are much more likely to be peopled by indigenous people than are larger churches. Why? There are many reasons. Sometimes indigenous people choose not to associate with non-indigenous folks out of fear, pride, or oversight. Non-indigenous people often don't want to live in or around indigenous cultures. Often indigenous people live by different values that don't encourage growth for growth's sake. They are more likely to value adherence to their tradition than openness to amalgamation. Sometimes indigenous and non-indigenous folks have never learned to dance the same dance and are a little leery of taking the first steps. For worship to be authentic, faithful, and effective in an indigenous community, it must understand, be respectful of, and draw on the indigenous rituals that have emerged from the people's shared history.

The newcomer to an indigenous community can expect that there are rituals in place for welcoming the newborn, rites of passage from childhood to adulthood, family making, crisis response, honoring elders, and celebrating death. Some of these will be within the religious community, some alongside, and some outside. The newcomer who seeks to lead an indigenous community will ignore, refute, or appropriate these rituals at his or her own peril. This newcomer who wishes to have a lengthy, rewarding, and effective ministry in such a community will have to learn the indigenous words and ways and give the people time to determine his or her suitability for adoption into the culture.

How can the indigenous ways be learned? Listen. Listen some more. Never stop listening. Sit down with trusted old timers and get them to list and describe all their traditions, annual events, holy places and objects, and religious and cultural practices. Identify every "holy" day in the church year and ask how it is observed. Study whatever historical records exist. Take college courses in anthropology and folk culture. Study the scriptures with the heart of an anthropologist and see the biblical record as the journals of indigenous peoples. Learn to speak the indigenous language and translate your theology and the denominational book of worship (the parts that are useful) into that language. Honor the people's desire to sing their own songs. Be respectful of traditional ways. Attend everything that happens in the indigenous community. Identify the ones who might be in the role of shaman in the community and try to apprentice. Plan to stick round and let people know you're not just passing through. Put yourself up for adoption into this indigenous culture. Rather than replace old customs with bright new ideas, let your new ventures be in fallow fields. Lay your ego aside and let an old-timer tailor your new ideas to their traditional ways. Lead by following and serving. Teach other newcomers everything you've learned. Encourage them to patiently seek adoption.

An indigenous community is not necessarily a closed community. Most of us live in a mobile, transitory society. People move to new places following jobs or their yellow brick roads. Adult children sometimes come home after learning new ways elsewhere. Indigenous people meet and try to accommodate to those from other cultures. It's good and possible for churches to be places and peoples where different cultures can seek to become "one in Christ." The old metaphor and style was to try being a melting pot. The new and better metaphor is to be like an Irish stew—rich and zesty with multiple tastes. Respect, sample, and interpret each other's indigenous ways. With permission and attribution, appropriate the ones with which all can identify. Invent new ones, abandoning those that don't click and retaining the ones that speak for all.

Questions:

1. Name as many indigenous customs and holy objects in your setting as you can.
2. How have these troubled or enriched your life in this place?

Suggestions:

1. As a church project or on your own, make a photo album of what is distinctive about your church's culture, or video your old timers telling their indigenous stories.
2. Plan a culture evening that shares the foods unique to your church, act out skits illustrating your indigenous practices, sing your people's songs, and so forth.

PRINCIPLE #7: Most Folks in Smaller Churches Would Rather Folk Dance than Watch a Ballet

The act of worship becomes a "folk dance" in slow motion, a graceful glid-
ing of people seeing the familiar and touching the friendly as they enter, take
their places, renew their sense of the Lord's loving care, and "depart in peace."[8]

Let me be clear about the distinction I'm drawing between folk dancing and
watching a ballet. The distinction is not about dance preferences. It's not about
the volume, tempo, or style of music. It's only partly about moving around
versus being still. And it's certainly not about being high-brow or low-brow.

So what is it about? It's about expectation and active involvement. While
attending the ballet, I expect to have an individual experience watching others
dance. At a folk dance I expect to be involved as one of the dancers. At the
ballet I expect to have an aesthetic watching and listening experience. I expect
a folk dance to be physical and sensual—oral, visual, tactile. At the ballet I
expect a mind experience with some heart. At a folk dance I expect to have a
heart and body experience, with some mind mixed in. At the ballet I expect to
leave inspired by the beauty and intellectually refreshed. At a folk dance I expect to leave invigorated, a little sweaty, physically refreshed and fatigued, so-
cially connected, emotionally and spiritually whole, and anxious to come again.

What makes the difference? One is individual; the other is communal and
creates a culture and a community. One is more passive and one is more active.
One is more formal and one is less formal. One is for spectators and one is
participatory and attracts people who want to do more than watch. One is safer
for timid people and one attracts people with the courage to go out on the floor.
With one, attendees watch and the ballet will go on without them. With the
other, the attendees are the dancers and are essential to the action.

Why is worship in a smaller church more likely to be a folk dance than a
ballet? Numbers account for one difference. A crowd can attend a ballet, but a
folk dance works best when there's enough room for everyone to be on the
floor and few enough people for everyone to see and hear. Strangers are more
likely to attend a ballet, knowing they don't have to interact. Most people at a
folk dance will have been there before or have come to meet other dancers.
They will know or soon know many of the others and even know the dancing
styles of at least some of the other dancers. Ballet is more of an age segregated
activity—children and youth take ballet lessons, those who attend are primarily
adults. Folk dances are most fun when they're intergenerational and attract
singles, doubles, and families. Folk dances attract social people who value inter-
dependency, community, learning from and teaching others. Finally, I suspect

that people who enjoy folk dancing and love to be actively involved will gravitate to a smaller church and people who prefer watching and listening to others will seek out a larger church.

So what does this mean for those who plan and lead the small church folk dance? It's not as easy as it looks, so learn the calls and how to coordinate with the music. Study the history of the dances, study the techniques, study the methodology of great callers. Prepare well, but be responsive and spontaneous. A good leader includes others in the leadership and doesn't hog the spotlight. Take time to orient and assimilate those new to the dance. Encourage the spectators to come out onto the floor. Encourage people to enjoy themselves and expect that they will. The dance will only have as much spirit as the caller and the musicians. Remember that the music is as important as the caller and that neither the musician nor the caller can work without the other. Remind the attendees that it's just folk music until they start dancing. Then it becomes folk dancing.

Take time to tell the stories behind the dances so everyone appreciates the tradition that supports them. Remember that the dance carries and communicates the culture from which it came. Dance both the old dances and the new ones. Remind people that the intent is enjoyment, not performance. Remember that most of your dancers are quite serious about their dancing, even as they are thoroughly enjoying themselves. Pace the dance—mix some fast with some slow, some simple with some more difficult, good beginning dances and good ending dances. Encourage interaction, not just dancing with one partner. And have refreshment breaks so the dancers can cool down and build relationships.

What does this have to do with smaller churches? Attending the ballet is a completely different activity from folk dancing. People who like one may not like the other. If you do things in the smaller church the way you'd do it with a folk dancing group, you will be on the right track to having worship that works in smaller settings.

Question:

Is your worship more like a folk dance or a ballet performance? How? Why? Which would you prefer? What other parallel would you use? Why?

Suggestions:

1. Attend a well known folk dance and watch the caller to see what you can learn about leading the liturgy.
2. Hold a folk dance for your church and then talk with your folks about the parallels.

PRINCIPLE # 8: Smaller Church Worship Is More a Public than a Private Experience

Ultimately, life goes better with a circle of friends. Without this circle of safety, it is extremely difficult to erase the fear.
—Patch Adams, M.D., *Gesundheit!* [9]

Patch Adams is a social revolutionary whose medical career has been devoted to helping people be healthy, whole, and happy, rather than merely fixing illness, and to giving away free health care. He and his revolutionary approach to health and medicine were popularized by Robin Williams in the movie *Patch Adams*.

He begins a chapter on self, family, community, and the world with three sentences: "The most distressing health problem for many people is the combination of boredom, fear, and loneliness. Our health is damaged most by loneliness and lovelessness. If relationships with our families, friends, and ourselves are not going well, no amount of physical health can compensate." [10] I believe this is true. Toward the end of nurturing and sustaining healthy persons and relationships, public worship—through its most effective rituals and liturgies—is a primary arena in our society for transforming boredom, fear, and loneliness into fascination, fearlessness, and camaraderie. Worship can address that which is of interest to the people, it can confront the fears that keep people awake at night, it can bring people together. Smaller communities of faith, where people matter and where relationships are primary can be an essential antidote to loneliness and lovelessness.

One of the ironic truths of group life generally and church life specifically is that the larger the group, one knows and is in relationship with fewer people. Carl Dudley makes two simple, profound, and related points. The first is this: "The small congregation is the appropriate size for only one purpose: the members can know one another personally." [11] I would argue that it is the right size for more than just this one purpose. Dudley's second point is: "In small churches, more people know more people, and know more about more people, than in most larger congregations." [12] The smaller a church is, the more likely it is to be a one-celled organism; the larger it is the more likely it is to be composed of many cells. The larger the congregation, the greater the probability that individuals will only know a select few. The smaller the congregation, the more relationships people will have and the more heterogeneous they often are. Quite possibly, the worshiper will know and be able to interact with most of those who are present.

People come to churches for different reasons. Some seek community, others want a private experience. Several years ago in Warwick, we were baptizing a young child. The child's grandmother came from New York for the occasion. After the service, she approached me with tears in her eyes and commented upon how meaningful the service had been; however, she also admitted to some distress. She commented on how connected our congregation was with one another and then recalled that many years before when she and her husband were looking for a church they would not have chosen a church like ours. She said they had wanted a church where they could sit in the back pew and be anonymous. There are folks who prefer anonymity because they are shy, overwhelmed, or emotionally or spiritually injured. Folks seeking anonymity may deliberately pass your smaller church by in order to get lost in a big church. For them, community will not be a motivating goal.

This raises a multi-faceted task for the smaller church in its worship. First, it has to market itself so that people seeking or willing to try a public worship experience will recognize that you offer it. Every Saturday, we have a small block ad in the local newspaper. In addition to our name, address, phone number, and time for worship, we include a descriptive phrase. One of the phrases we use is "A Small Church with a Big Heart." Another is "A Hospitable People." We intend that these phrases will communicate that our church is compassionate and our worship is safe and open to all.

A second task is to offer public worship that is not invasive or threatening to visitors and introverts, but will draw them slowly and safely into the public arena. For this reason, we put clear windows in the wall between our narthex and sanctuary, so that visitors can see the sanctuary and people before they enter. I don't ask visitors to stand and introduce themselves or put them on the spot in any way. A church that understands the depth of true hospitality understands that genuine hospitality allows people to be themselves and to blossom publicly at their own pace. For example, a carefully planned and clearly laid out bulletin with a participatory liturgy helps the new and uninitiated know what's coming next and gives them the opportunity to hear their voice along side the voices of the congregation. To find one's public voice in a safe worship environment is the first step toward finding voice in other, more public and possibly threatening settings. Smaller church worship can and should be a safe and painless initiation into the Community of God.

A third task is to educate the congregation concerning the difference between meditation and worship. One person can meditate; it takes two or more to worship. Worship is, by definition, a public act, the work of all the people. The words and actions of the liturgy should be more public than private. Many laity and quite a few pastors don't understand this difference. The education happens as the people experience and become cognizant of the communal, participatory nature of their worship experience.

A fourth task for the worship leader is to see that the focus and integrity of worship is not distorted or diverted, to monitor the pace and time, to insure that no one dominates, and to see that worship does not become a forum for pet peeves and personal agendas. A few years ago, a member of our congregation was being evicted from our church's affordable housing complex. This person was quite angry and used our joys and concerns time on several occasions to strongly criticize the housing management. Outside of worship, several of us were able to listen to her with compassion while we helped her understand that the spirit of sanctuary in our worship was being trespassed by her angry attacks. She was able to stay with us through this difficult time in her life.

The final and most important task of public worship is to worship so that God is well praised, the people are well served, and God's community leaves connected and strengthened for their life of discipleship. This requires intentionality and coordination. It's easier to perform a semblance of worship for a passive audience. All they have to do is be quiet, show some respect, and foot the bill.

My son, the basketball player, has educated me about the two styles of basketball played in the National Basketball Association. One style is to draw the defense all onto one side of the floor while the best, most athletic shooter seeks to maneuver, freelance, and score. The other way is to have a coordinated, choreographed offense that utilizes the whole team in moving the ball faster than the defense is able to move their bodies until one player is free to take a high percentage shot. The latter is more work and takes more practice. Translated into the world of worship, this is the public style of worship at its best.

When worship is coordinated and choreographed, everyone is drawn into the action. Each worshiper understands how the game is being played and what the goal is. The initiative flows back and forth throughout the community of worshipers. Each passing of the ball involves the whole team and moves the worship closer to its climax. When the worship ends, all the worshipers have the satisfaction of knowing they were part of the action and integral to the process.

Your public and participatory worship can take advantage of your size to more faithfully and effectively love God and one another toward the realization and strengthening of the Community of God. This is the antidote to the loneliness and lovelessness of which Patch Adams wrote. To incarnate this is our most difficult and important task. Rainer Maria Rilke wrote: "For one human to love another: that is perhaps the most difficult of all of our tasks, the ultimate, the last test and proof, the work for which all other work is but preparation."[13] This is the work of the people.

Question:

Is your church more of a public or private experience? What might be done to make it more public, more the work of the people? What would help your people embrace this movement?

Invite your whole church (if it's fairly small) to a large, comfortable living room, with a big screen TV, make lots of popcorn, and watch the video *Patch Adams*. Then talk about (over more popcorn and beverages) the parallels between the medical world and the church world, Patch Adams's approach and your church. Ask if they can see themselves as an alternative to rigid organizational styles and as an antidote for some of the loneliness and sickness in our society. Explore how their worship can contribute to this alternative antidote.

PRINCIPLE # 9: Worship in Smaller Churches Is a Family Reunion

> Return to old watering holes for more than water—
> friends and dreams are there to meet you.
> —African Proverb[14]

Family reunions are fascinating rituals. Once a year a family clan will rent a hall, reserve a recreation area, or come back to the family homestead. The people of each generation who claim this as their family come from near and far to renew common ties. When they gather, family news is updated, changes are noted, babies are welcomed, new spouses are confirmed, departed members are remembered and mourned, family stories are told and embellished, feuds are resolved and exacerbated, indigenous rituals are observed. Though not much new happens, everyone goes home with roots, identity, and place in the family clarified and solidified.

Worship in small churches is a family reunion and more. People of various generations, who behave like an extended family and are connected by accident, choice, or blood come together to worship their heavenly Parent, identify who is present and absent, exchange greetings and regrets, receive and pass on good news and bad, baptize and confirm, marry and bury, pray and eat, and practice the rituals that tell them whose they are, who they are, where they belong, and what they need to be doing. This familial nature of their worship is one of the distinctive features of small churches.[15]

More and more of us in this increasingly rootless time live at great geographical or emotional distance from family. My parents are both dead, my one sibling lives many miles away, the rest of the Rays and all of my wife's family live more than a thousand miles away. If it had not been for the members of four small churches who have been very much family for us, my wife, children, and I would have lived an orphan existence. We are not unusual. Many in our churches are devoid of family due to such realities as distance, divorce, or death. Luckily, no one in a smaller church is too insignificant or young to experience its familial nature. Six-year-old Sarah in my first church queried her mother: "All the people at church are part of *our* family, aren't they?" Yes, Sarah, when we are at our best, they are.

The familial nature of smaller churches is experienced through their shared life, but it's in their liturgical life that the familial relationship is ritualized and receives its power. Roy Rappaport, in *Ecology, Meaning, and Religion*, identified the importance of ritual in establishing familial relationship: "Anthropology has known since Durkeim's time that rituals establish or enhance solidarity among those joining in their performance."[16] There's little doubt that this phenomenon happens in smaller, healthy congregations. This is more difficult in larger churches where there is less intimacy and where relationships tend to be more formal and less intergenerational. But the question is: Why are these familial dynamics so present and how can our liturgies and rituals give them greater substance and reliability?

Religious language is saturated with family imagery—Father God, Mother Mary, Jesus the Son, and in the Roman Catholic tradition, Father priest, Sister nun, and Brother monk—which contributes to the familial nature of the Church. We use familial terminology to name who we are and what we do—the church family, family night, the communion table is sometimes called the family table, and, in some traditions, men and women are called Brother so-and-so and Sister-so-and-so. We even have a family bath ritual in the Church—baptism. The family experience happens because churches do the kinds of things families do. We have family meetings. We have family dinners. We play together the way families do. The church children play together the way siblings and cousins play. The shared life of smaller churches is very much a tribal or clan-like experience.

If worship is truly a family reunion, then the whole family should be present. Churches may have simultaneous worship and education hours as a convenience, but they sacrifice much in the process. Adults who worship regularly but do not study may end up being pious but not literate in the faith. Children who study but don't worship may know something about their religion but not know how to experience the presence of God. It's been said that Jesus played with children and taught adults, while today's church tries to teach its children while it plays with its adults. I commend those churches who are still willing to come together long enough to worship and study together. Even more, I applaud those churches who have found or remembered how to worship together as one large, extended family of all ages.

Some churches have found that when they provide a box of stuffed animals or boxes of crayons and children's bulletins that their children are quite content to remain in worship, benefiting from worship both subliminally and actually. In Warwick, we had education before worship for all ages and child care during worship for only the very youngest. That church was a close enough family that all adults were welcome to discipline the church's children whenever a little loving correction was needed.

The best recipe for keeping the whole church family together for worship is working to make worship enough of a sensual treat that neither children nor adults distract one another, act up, or get fussy. Shorter sermons that use more story than analysis, songs and hymns for children as well as adults, liturgy with words that communicate to all ages, movement that makes worship both a spirit and body experience, symbols and images that spark the imagination, and sacraments that emphasize their physicality and are this worldly rather than other worldly are all ways of making the worship hour a family reunion.

In San Rafael, our sacramental life strengthens the family tie. We conduct baptisms before our children leave worship for church school (yes, our church still sends it's children out to church school after our storytelling time). Sometimes children are encouraged to gather around the font for baptisms. I remind young and old that part of the meaning of baptism is that the one being baptized is being initiated into both the Family of God and our church family. The one being baptized is identified for the children and adults as a new brother or sister, son or daughter. Children could be given paper and markers and invited to make welcome cards for their newly baptized sister or brother. At every baptism of a child, the congregation sings to the tune "Morning Has Broken," a song that names a child and sings a prayer on his or her behalf:

(Name) we name you: And with thanksgiving,
Offer our prayer and sing you this song.
We are the church, your spiritual family.
Sing we our praises to Christ the Lord.

Children we all are, of God the creator;
Risking and loving, daring to see
The heavenly kingdom growing among us.
Sing we our praises to Christ the Lord.

I explicitly identify the communion table as the family table for all God's Family, including our children. After the sermon, our children return to the sanctuary and are a very present part of the family circle around our family table. It is an affront to exclude children from the Lord's Table and our family meal when there is no record of Jesus ever excluding children (or anyone) from anything. Referring to communion as a profound mystery, John Westerhoff writes in *Bringing Up Children in the Christian Faith*: "When we argue that children do not know enough to receive the Sacrament of Holy Communion, we seem to forget that perhaps children are the only ones who can fully understand its significance."[17]

We need to remember that our church families, like our personal families, include more than those currently comprising the family. They also include those who came before us and those who will come after us. Communion is a wonderful time for celebrating the whole Family of God of all times and places. During our World Communion Sunday service we remember the whole human family. I often arrange to use a variety of breads from different cultures. On this occasion, I urge people to bring and name those loved ones to the table who are not physically present. People have brought deceased children, spouses, parents, saints of our church—and large lumps in the throat.

Every season of the Church year presents opportunities for liturgical family reunion:

- Advent and Christmas provide obvious family events, from Advent workshops to decorate the sanctuary, to Advent wreath liturgies, to Christmas Eve pageants and family services.
- Epiphany recalls the flight of Jesus' family to Egypt and the baptism of Jesus and can include a Twelfth Night party.
- Lent can begin with a Shrove or Fat Tuesday party and include opportunities for intergenerational study and worship. A Maundy Thursday liturgy in the form of an authentic Jewish seder has specific responsibilities for children. Good Friday includes the memory that Jesus did not die before seeing that his mother would be cared for and the realization that Jesus had included all those who loved him in his family and was willing to give his life for the least of these.
- Christ's Easter appearances were to those who loved him as family. Our Easter service always includes our children giving a jelly bean (reminiscent of an Easter egg) to all the adults with the ancient greeting, "Christ is risen," to which the adults respond, "He is risen indeed!"
- Pentecost celebrates the extension of the Christian family to diverse people of many cultures.
- Within the liturgical life of our smaller churches, we can celebrate the birthdays of those who have no one else who will remember.
- On Memorial Day Sunday and around All Saints Day, we can remember the anniversaries of the deaths of loved ones in the congregation.
- One Valentine's Day Sunday, we designed a whole worship service around love stories.
- Children's Sabbath and graduation days can be celebrated.

Recently, my favorite aunt Elizabeth died. Almost the whole Ray clan gathered in Colorado for her memorial service. It was a wonderful celebration of her life of faithfulness and a wonderful reunion of an extended family, some of whom had drifted out of touch. Similarly, some of my finest worship experiences have been memorial services of church members. When members of a church marry, the whole church can turn the occasion into a wonderful celebration of family formation. Churches overlook extraordinary ritual and liturgical opportunities when they only focus on their weekly worship. Any time the Church or representatives of the Church convene families for family ritual and liturgy, there is the opportunity for family reunion and transformation.

In smaller churches and particularly in their worship, the reality of family is poignant and precious. Worship in smaller churches is very much a family reunion. In our family celebrations, we are reminded that our old give our young a history and tradition. The young give our old hope and a future. Each generation in the family is a link in the chain of faithfulness that must be preserved and strengthened. Together we embody the whole Family of God. There is truth and power in the old adage that the family that prays and worships together, stays together.

Questions:

1. How is the idea of worship as a family reunion experienced in your church?
2. How might your church make its worship times more of a reunion of the whole family?

Suggestions:

1. If you've not been to a real family reunion, try to wangle an invitation from one of your church members to one of theirs. If successful in getting invited, observe the reunion with the eye of an anthropologist.
2. Ask a group to draw the floor plan of your sanctuary. Then jot the initials of where as many people as you can remember generally sit. Draw circles (halos) for where now departed saints used to sit. Draw solid lines between those who are related by blood or long-standing friendship. Draw a hyphenated line between those who work together in the life of the church. Draw a dotted line between those who have a ruptured relationship. Who is out of relationship? What strategies would put more lines into your sketch?

PRINCIPLE #10: Smaller Church Worship Is a Time for Social Caring and Building Community

A contemporary Hasidic rabbi asked his disciple: "How is Moshe Yaakov doing?" The disciple didn't know. "What!" shouted the Rabbi, "You don't know? You pray under the same roof with him, you study the same texts, you serve the same God, you sing the same songs, and you dare to tell me that you don't know whether Moshe Yaakov is in good health, whether he needs help, advice, or comforting.[18]

Why is it so hard to get our San Rafael worshipers out of the courtyard and narthex and into the sanctuary in time for the prelude? Is it because the prelude isn't worth hearing? Not at all. Is it because they prefer to chat than to join the silence? I don't think so? Is it because they really don't care much about worshiping? Not at all. Rather, I think it's because after a week or so of eventful living and being apart from one another, worship feels superficial and artificial if they haven't first checked in with and checked up on one another. I think it's because their ritual of worship so depends on social caring and community building that they can't worship without it. They understand and believe John Donne's famous words in his *Devotions*:

> No man is an Iland, intire of it selfe; every man is a peece of the
> Continent, a part of the maine, if a Clod bee washed away by the Sea,
> Europe is the lesse, as well as if a Promontorie were, as well as if a Mannor
> of they friends or If thine owne were; any mans death diminishes me,
> because I am involved in Mankinde; And therefore never send to know
> for whom the bell tolls; it tolls for thee.

Worship in larger churches is more of an individual experience than in smaller churches. People come looking for sustenance for their living, but most of their living is separate from the others worshiping in the same space. The "Clods," with whom they are involved and for whom they care, are mostly somewhere else. In smaller congregations, where most of the people have spent years together, or where the church is in a small town or rural setting so people see each other outside of church, or where there is a conscious effort to build a sense of community, people can't worship until they know every Clod is in place, and they know the condition of the Clods who are absent.

Does authentic Christian worship depend on and require community? Trends in our turn-of-the-century church assume not. Church growth literature contain few if any cautionary notes about the loss of community when corporate worship turns into mass inspirational events and congregations of a few hundred turn into religious institutions of thousands. Few theologians and church bureaucrats would venture to name a number beyond which a church ceases to be a church and becomes an institution.

Biblical and historical theology believe community is essential, even required, for Christian churches. Psalm 133, from the Hebrew hymn book and the source book for much of Christian worship, reminds us: "How very good and pleasant it is when kindred live together in unity! . . . For there the Lord ordained his blessing, life forevermore." Rephrase this in the negative and its truth is more obvious: "How very bad and unpleasant it is when those out of relationship exist separate from one another! . . . For the Lord has not ordained or blessed this and it will not last long."

I believe that when Jesus said, "Where two or three are gathered in my name, I am there among them" (Mt. 18:20), he was implying that he was especially there because in small numbers there is greater probability of community and where there is community there is Christ.

Paul's first letter to the Corinthian church is a warning to a church that was growing beyond the optimum size for community. He chides them in chapter 11 for ignoring the communal essence of the Lord's Supper. In chapter twelve he establishes the standard for Christian community: "But God has so arranged the body . . . that there may be no dissension within the body, but the members may have the same care for one another. If one member suffers, all suffer together with it; if one member is honored, all rejoice together with it" (I Cor. 12:24–26). Chapter 13 is Paul's beautiful hymn to love which claims that love is the essence and ultimate in life together, and it would be almost impossible to demonstrate that there can be genuine love outside of community.

Paul Hanson's exhaustive study of the development of community in the Bible, *The People Called*, identifies community as a primary thread woven through scripture from Genesis to Revelation:

> The entire history of the biblical notion of community . . . finds its final unity and focus in worship of the one true God. From that center alone, it derives its understanding of what is true, just, and good, along with the courage and power to stand on the side of truth and justice, whatever the cost.
>
> The notion of community thus arising from our biblical heritage has a potentially profound contribution to make to a threatened world groping for direction.[19]

If community was normative in biblical times for the entire Judeo-Christian faith community, does it remain so? Is community merely a nice idea or is it God's prerequisite for a Christian church, even today? Most commentators on the church, if pressed hard and pushed to the wall, would probably say it is not a prerequisite. I believe it still is.

Dietrich Bonhoeffer, a giant among twentieth century theologians, asserted that Christianity is synonymous with community: "Christianity means community through Jesus Christ and in Jesus Christ. No Christian community is more or less than this."[20] If *Christianity means community*, pure and simple, then one person alone cannot be or remain Christian and a crowd too large for real community has ceased being a Christian church. If this radical notion is true, then building, being, and sustaining community is the principle calling of the Christian Church and the quality that the world most needs from the Church. The Christian Church, which then is interchangeable with the Christian Community, becomes the prototype and precursor of the Community of God, God's vision for the whole created order. These claims, if true, are close to unfathomable and are extraordinarily tantalizing.

Elizabeth O'Connor spent the last fifty years chronicling the very remarkable story of the Church of the Savior in Washington, D.C. They have taken the concept of Christian Community so seriously that when the church grew to about eighty members, the congregation accepted the challenge of their founder and pastor, Gordon Cosby, that they were too large and divided into eight small house mission churches. Elizabeth O' Connor's legacy could rest on this statement: "There is no higher achievement in all the world than to be a person in community, and this is the call of every Christian. We are to be builders of liberating communities that free love in us and free love in others."[21] Maybe it wasn't hyperbole when T. S. Eliot wrote the lines that began this book: "There is no life that is not in community,/And no community not lived in praise of God."[22]

So, if we accept that community is the principle calling of the church, how can we encourage deeper social caring and community when we gather to worship? First, let's not presume that real social caring and community and worship wait until the people gather in the sanctuary or that it ends when they leave it. Particularly in smaller churches, social caring, community building, and the first steps of the folk dance worship begin when the first two worshipers spot one another in the parking lot and ends when the last two leave. So, create an atmosphere and space that's conducive for the initial, fundamental and lasting expression of caring and community. Maybe we should be less insistent on starting and ending on time. Perhaps it's a sacrilege to omit a coffee hour or social time. Imagine that the whole worship experience is like a sandwich. If the liturgy (from prelude to postlude) is the filling, the sandwich is sure to fall apart if there's no bread to hold it together. The bread is everything that happens before and after the beginning and closing music. In some churches the bread is day-old, tasteless Wonder Bread. In others, it is a rich, tasty custom made loaf that fills and nourishes.

Do what you can to create a worship space that is warm, inviting, and conducive to community building. You know those places that feel warm and hospitable and those places that are cold and repelling. Warm colors, lovely flowers, sufficient but not glaring lighting, padded pews or chairs, attractive symbolism, space that is designed to human scale (rather than too spacious or cramped) all contribute to an inviting environment. Do your best to see that everything isn't screwed down and that all the floor space isn't occupied with furniture. The people can't become a community if they can't get to one another or touch another.

Nurture a core of courageous people who are conscientious about establishing a caring worship environment within the congregation. These people should be on the lookout for newcomers and people who appear distressed. They should be ready to sit in proximity with those who appear lonely. They should be quick to share a hymnal, pass a Kleenex, cuddle a troubled child, or greet the returning dropout.

Music is key. Does it elevate or suppress the spirit? Does the singing feel like a gathering around a piano or solitary voices in the wilderness? The words and melody can encourage or inhibit community. "Blest Be the Tie that Binds" does this better than "In the Garden Alone." Does the choir intend to perform and entertain, or reach out to, embrace, and encourage the rest of the people? Every favorite hymn was once new, but too many new hymns or songs may encourage people to clam up and drop out.

The liturgy is crucial. Does your congregation experience it as a random barrage of rote words or as a carefully crafted script that names, defines, and dramatizes the communal vision of the Gospel? I often spend as much time and thought on the liturgy that is the order of worship as I do on the sermon. I do this because I think it's just as important, sometimes more so. The words "we" and "our" dominate the bulletin. "I" and "my" are almost impossible to find. (Have you noticed the language of the Lord's Prayer is "our" language, not "my" language?) The majority of our worship hour is multiple voices singing and speaking with one another and people praying together—silently and out loud. Less than half the time, one person speaks while others listen. The liturgy is more than words said or spoken. The liturgy is the script for the rituals. There should be some time in the liturgy when the people are encouraged to greet one another. Their active greetings both symbolize and create community. The liturgy can encourage and facilitate other opportunities for movement and make worship more than an auditory and visual experience.

If Paul Hanson is correct that the dominant theme of scripture is community, then the use of scripture and our proclamation based upon it (the sermon) ought to also speak of community in all its nuance and possibility. If we accept as gospel the doctrine of the priesthood of all believers, a fundamental in my Baptist and Congregational heritage, then the people in the pews should have something to proclaim in addition or response to the words of the preacher. How can we facilitate their contribution to the Gospel message of social caring and community building?

Probably the time in our worship when our community is most deepened and broadened is in our sharing of joys and concerns and time of prayer. News is shared. People have a chance to be heard. Consciousness is raised. People volunteer to help. Issues are identified. Prayers are focused. We really do both grieve and celebrate with one another. Then we are equipped to offer ourselves to God in prayer around all this material. In San Rafael we end our time of prayer by singing the very familiar and loved refrain "And God will raise you up on eagles' wings."[23]

My philosophical twenty-one year old son, who questions everything, is furious with me if I leave this refrain out of our liturgy. I think that's because he senses along with the rest of us that it is the whole community of us that God is raising up on eagle's wings. In that is truth and strength and possibility.

The test for everything we do in worship is this: does it build, detract from, or prevent the formation and expression of the Community of God in this place? When everything is measured by that question, Christian Community will inevitably grow.

Questions:

1. Do you think that when Jesus said, "Where two or three are gathered in my name, I am there among them," that he meant to say he would even be there or that he would especially be there?
2. Do you agree with Bonhoeffer that "Christianity means community" and with Eliot that there is "no community not lived in praise of God?" What would your congregation be like if it took these ideas very seriously?

Suggestions:

1. Preach one or more sermons on Christian community and have a sermon feed back time or a study group on the theme.
2. Gather some people to help you measure everything that happens in worship, from arrival to departure, by the test of whether it builds, detracts from, or prevents social caring and community.

PRINCIPLE #11: Worship in Smaller Churches Is More Emotional

> The best and most beautiful things in the world cannot be seen or even touched. They must be felt with the heart.
> —Helen Keller

> You think too much, that is your trouble.
> Clever people and grocers, they weigh everything.
> —Zorba the Greek

Picture a smaller number of people in smaller worship spaces and compare them to their counterparts in larger sanctuaries. More often than not, those who make up the smaller group have been worshiping in that place longer, are attached to one special pew, have more of an attachment to other aspects of the space, know more people well and know most of the other people, have been more personally involved in maintaining the place and keeping it open, and have experienced the life passage rituals of family and close friends in that space. Many of the losses and gains of their lives will be associated with that room. With this kind of history, these folks are likely to have poignant memories and meanings related to everything around them. That worship space will be a three-dimensional living album of the emotional times of their lives. Just to be there is an experience that touches the heart even more than it enlightens the mind.

But it's more than the power of the space that sparks the emotions. If I say the same thing in the same way to you at a distance of twenty feet, I'm likely to get twice the reaction from you than if I say it from forty feet away. While I may not show it, I'm likely to have twice the reaction to what happens in a group of ten people I know well than if I'm in a group of twenty with whom I am only acquainted. I will probably laugh louder or have tears well up easily or have my face flush in anger more readily in the smaller, better known group. Small numbers and close proximity breed greater vulnerability. Intimacy is the seedbed of emotion.

Worship with fewer than one hundred will be more emotional for more people than worship with a larger number. If it were possible to tally and keep track of such things, it's likely there will be far more tears shed, laughs laughed, angry outbursts, joyful responses, feelings hurt, and love expressed in a smaller church than a larger one. Not only will there be more emotionalism, but there will be opposite reactions to it. Some will try even harder to control their emotions with people they know well and others will feel freer to let their emotions go. In general, in a smaller setting, people will feel freer to be themselves, and this makes all the difference in their worship and their lives.

Traditional educational experiences tend to be experiences of the mind with the heart playing a supporting role. Worship experiences tend to be experiences of the heart with the mind playing the supporting role. Take hymn choices, for example. Many pastors pick hymns for their lyrics and their theology. We think it's a good hymn to sing if the words articulate the thought and theology we want to impart. Most people in the pew want to sing the hymns they've sung their whole lives, the hymns they associate with memorable events, the hymns with wonderful melodies, and the hymns that make them feel good. If they cause the toe to tap, all the better. Take Russ, for example. Russ is one of the smartest people I know. He's an engineer who travels all over the world designing and building pharmaceutical plants. Russ is serious about his church and faith. Russ really dislikes our new hymnal. For him, there are too many new hymns and too many new words to old hymns. Russ wants to sing the old, old story in the old, old way. He's not alone in that, either. If I want Russ to have an enriching and transforming worship experience, then I better make sure he and those like him get to sing at least one familiar favorite each Sunday.

One common conflict in churches concerns the singing of Christmas carols. Seminary training and books of worship have educated worship leaders to sing Advent hymns during the four weeks of Advent and Christmas carols on Christmas Eve and the following two weeks. This notion only makes sense to the clergy, the theologians, and those who elevate thought over feelings. The problem is magnified by the fact that there aren't enough familiar and loved Advent hymns to spread over four weeks. And there are more loved Christmas carols than can be sung in the three services where they're allowed. Do we really think anyone's Advent will be wrecked if we let them sing "Silent Night" on the second Sunday of Advent? Advent-Christmas is an emotional season, so why not sing emotional music? I balance Advent and Christmas music and tip the balance the third and fourth week of Advent.

In San Rafael, some of us really like the new hymnal and some don't like it much at all. The only time there's been open rebellion was the first Advent-Christmas season that we had the new hymnal. In the interest of inclusive language and updating archaic language, many of the lyrics of well-known carols were changed in the new hymnal. People opened their mouths to sing lyrics from the heart they've been singing since they were in the cradle. Others sang the lyrics as printed in the hymnal. The result was confusion, consternation, and complaints. The answer was reasonable compromise. We now sing out of the old hymnal during Advent and Christmas and out of the new hymnal the rest of the year. Many people are happier, and no one has been harmed. Our response to the music is an example of the emotional power inherent in our worship experience.

Music is only one place in worship where emotion is felt. Just being in the presence of particular others can be emotional. In Shrewsbury, the church lived and worshiped through a bitter, year-long community fight over whether to build a new addition to the local elementary school. The community was evenly divided over this issue, and the tension was palpable in the church. It took two community votes to decide the issue, still by only about a ten vote margin. While the overt expression of disagreement was checked at the door, the emotional feelings were still in the room. In an effort to bring reconciliation to the community and healing to the church after the final vote, the church conducted a community wide service of reconciliation.

I've worked hard to resurrect the Middle Ages' concept of sanctuary. Historically, when individuals were in the church sanctuary, they could not be apprehended or arrested. Today, in the sanctuary of the worship hour and space, everyone should be free to be present, be free from assault, be free to feel and honor whatever emotions well up, be free to experience the graces of God and, hopefully, the acceptance of brothers and sisters in Christ. There are few places in our culture where emotions are considered acceptable. The sanctuary and faith community is one of those places. Pastors who are uncomfortable with emotionality might be better suited for pastoring and leading worship in larger congregations.

Tom Driver has written helpfully about the relationship between emotion and ritual. One of the contributions of ritual is that it provides place and control for emotionality:

> Ritual controls emotion while releasing it, and guides it while letting it run. Even in a time of grief, ritual lets joy be present through the permission to cry, lets tears become laughter, if they will, by making place for the fullness of tears' intensity—all this in the presence of communal assertiveness.
>
> A ritual is a party at which emotions are welcome. If the emotions are too strong, threatening to swamp the party, the ritual scenario can be used to guide and moderate them; and if the emotions are too weak, draining the event of its energy, the ritual can invoke them, like spirits, to be present, through the use of rhythm, display, and other summoning techniques. Any ritual performance is an invitation for energies to come together, to multiply their power by fusion.[24]

We see the connection between emotion and ritual most clearly and helpfully in wedding and death rituals. Through experience, people generally know what to expect and what the limits and possibilities are. Within the wedding experience and ritual, there is room for tears of loss and tears of joy, sentimentality and giddiness, resentment and gratitude, fear of what is ahead, and consummating love. The rituals of death offer the same range of possibilities. One of the first important tests of a new pastor is how she or he handles the first funeral. Will he say the right words? Will she be able to handle the surprises that the experience of death often elicits? Will he be appropriately empathetic and caring? People associate emotionality with religious rituals and expect that those who fill the priestly role will be able to manage that which threatens to overwhelm and facilitate healing of emotions.

Worship rituals should neither pander to emotionality nor seek to prevent it. They should embrace the whole human personality—mind, body, spirit, and emotions. This can happen naturally and effectively in our smaller congregations.

Questions:

1. What emotions do you experience yourself and witness in others within the realm of worship in your church?
2. Does your congregation try to repress, facilitate, or manipulate emotionality?

Suggestion:

Gather some people to discuss the role emotions play in your congregation. Carefully give examples and tell stories. Name the emotion-laden rituals that are unique or common to your church.

PRINCIPLE #12 It's Folly They Don't Like, Not Change

Story: The new pastor of the church thought the sanctuary was too dark. She began promoting the idea of a new chandelier. In sermons, in meetings, in the newsletter, around town, she talked about the chandelier. At the church meeting she called to decide on the chandelier, discussion went back and forth. Finally, the church patriarch stood and spoke the last word: "I don't think we need a chandelier! We can't afford one! We've gotten along just fine without one! We don't have any place to put one! And besides, nobody here knows how to play one!" He and the rest all voted a resounding "No." The idea of buying a chandelier was dropped.

Conventional wisdom says that smaller churches are more resistant to change than larger ones. A second piece of conventional wisdom says pastors shouldn't change anything for at least a year, particularly not the worship service or space. I don't believe the first and have never followed the second. That does not mean I'm cavalier or revolutionary about disrupting the way things are. Smaller churches that may have fewer resources with which to take risks, that may see themselves as caretakers of precious traditions, and that are probably more pragmatic because survival may have been a hard-fought struggle will carefully test what they say yes or no to. If an innovation is a dumb idea, they will probably call it a dumb idea and say no. If something is a new idea, they will probably want time to get used to it and would prefer to try it before committing to it. But that's different than being opposed to change when the risk is minimal or the benefits are real.

Consider the chandelier story. The patriarch was not opposed to change. He just thought the change should make sense and fill a need. Obviously the pastor did a poor job of communicating. She forgot to line up the leadership before calling for a decision. She was content to promote her own idea rather than planting the seed so the solution to the darkness could come from a trusted source within the congregation. Apparently, sanctuary darkness wasn't a commonly perceived problem and there had been no consideration of all possible solutions. Most serious of all, she probably squandered her credit line of trust and good will by pushing her ill-conceived innovation.

Each of the four very different small churches I have served was responsive to reasonable change from the beginning. Many of the changes were in the realm of worship. The goal was always to increase the vitality and meaning in the worship life of the congregation, without great cost, serious disruption, or rejection of holy practices or objects. In each church I soon introduced a different order of worship. In each case the new order replaced one in which no one had an investment. The new one was introduced with a clear rationale as to why I thought it was preferable. In each church, I quickly introduced a new bulletin format, one that was more attractive, easy to follow, flexible, and thoughtful. In each setting the expectation was established that there would be variety in the church's worship. There was not a ripple of opposition, and as Carl Nordstedt said, "At least he keeps us awake!"

I made one significant mistake in Warwick. There was a picture on the wall of Jesus in Gethsemane which I considered rather noxious. When we started remodeling, the picture quietly found its way into a closet, where I hoped it would never see the light of day. It wasn't long before our most respected pillar, Charlie Morse, asked, "What happened to the picture of Jesus?" Red faced, I admitted the picture was in the closet. We hung the picture over the mantle in the entry to the sanctuary. Charlie was satisfied and he affirmed or tolerated every other change.

Charlie was a key player in another of my newfangled notions. Some of my sermon ideas emerge rather late in the week. One Saturday afternoon, driving in the western Massachusetts hills, I was inspired by the connection between the Genesis creation story and our own creativity. I could simply talk about creativity or I could give people the opportunity to actually create within the context of worship. A trip to the art supply store produced a hunk of modeling clay. This was cut into two inch squares and placed on pieces of wax paper. As I considered how all this would play out, I had the fervent hope that Charlie Morse would pick that Sunday to be absent. He was present. The clay was passed out at the beginning of the sermon and the worshipers were encouraged to create while I preached. I told them that if they couldn't both create and listen, it was all right to just create. Charlie appeared busy throughout the sermon. After worship, all the creations were displayed on the parlor table. Charlie was proud of his. I thought it was the most creative of all. Charlie's wife scolded him for getting clay on his suit.

Far from being opposed to change, many smaller churches embrace and are often desperate for change, for something worth staying awake for, for alternatives to that which isn't working, for signs of new life. I believe pastors are expected to be leaders and leaders are expected to facilitate appropriate change; therefore, I try to lead carefully, respectfully, wisely, and not as the Lone Ranger.

I'm in my eighth year in San Rafael. By the end of the first year, it was clear we had building problems and a sanctuary in serious need of upgrading. The congregation tackled the whole project in stages, leaving the sanctuary until the end. We worked with a fine architect. We listened to everyone's ideas and accommodated as many as possible. Being an impatient person, I exercised all the patience I could muster, and we proceeded step by step. No one, including me, got their way on everything. We now have a completely renovated facility and a very different and extraordinary space for worship.

Through thirty years of parish ministry, I've learned some strategies for effective change:

- Change the little, easy, sure-fire things first, so that people's trust and appetite for change grow.
- Help people realize mistakes and failure is all right. Not every change works or lasts forever.
- Work constantly at elevating morale. People are much more accepting when they are feeling good about themselves and their church.
- Remind people that everything that is now accepted was once a new idea and that virtually no good idea was originally affirmed by everyone.

- Encourage people not to expect to like everything that happens. All that is reasonable for any of us is to like most things, most of the time.
- Fifty-one percent is not enough of a mandate for a change. Talk about the proposal, try to accommodate people's strongest wishes, insure that people's deepest concerns are heard, and compromise until you have achieved near consensus.
- Whenever possible and helpful, consider expert advice.
- Measure the realistic cost (tangible and intangible), and commit yourself to not leave the congregation to pick up the pieces on their own.
- Whenever possible, test the idea before committing to it. In two churches we experimented with changing the pew arrangement. In one case the change became permanent. In the other case we changed back.
- Do your best to have the ideas come from someone else. A wise pastor creates an environment in which most ideas come from other people.
- When you change one thing, leave other important things un-changed. It's human nature to look to the church for some stability and security.
- Actively love the people, whether you like each other's ideas or not.
- Unless the ship is actually sinking, some things are more important than change.

In regard to worship and its environment, find out first what is considered holy. Ask your leaders what is sacred and untouchable. Earn your people's trust and trust them in return. Remember, that which doesn't mean anything to you may well mean a lot to someone else. Don't change things for the sake of change; have a good reason and a clear rationale. Generally, it's better to start with little changes. Whenever possible, try a change for a few weeks and then decide together whether the change should be permanent. It's better to sup-port the ideas of others than to impose or push your own. If you choose one thing, leave other things alone. Help people understand this fundamental prin-ciple: until death us do change; after death nothing changes. Therefore, to resist all change is to be spiritually and mentally dead.

Questions:

1. Is change feared, accepted, or relished in your church? How does change most successfully happen there?

2. What rules for effective change would you add to the author's list?
3. What changes are needed in your worship life? What difference would that change make in the life of your people? Who needs to agree to make change most acceptable?

Suggestion:

Gather some people and ask each to share their personal history regarding change. Talk about the church's history with change. Then talk about what changes different ones of them would like to see in worship and church life. Imagine them, evaluate them, winnow them, prioritize them. Start with one or two of the easiest, most interesting, most popular, or most important ideas.

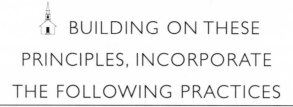

FOUR

BUILDING ON THESE PRINCIPLES, INCORPORATE THE FOLLOWING PRACTICES

PRACTICE #1: Design Every Part of Smaller Church Worship for the Number Expected

Groups of thirty-five, seventy-five, two hundred, and one thousand are as different from one another as an ant is from an eagle is from a cow is from a whale.[1]

The previous twelve principles were more about the fundamentals a person should understand as they plan for the worship life of a smaller church. The remaining practices lean toward the application side, and what should be done to provide faithful and effective worship for smaller numbers. The first of these is so obvious that it's easily forgotten: plan specifically for the number of worshipers you expect.

Consider parallels from the sports world. Tennis works best with singles or doubles on the court. Five per team seems to be the optimum number for basketball, given the rules, the size of the court, the fact that only one ball and two baskets are used. Those who created and developed football experimented with various team sizes. After all the experimentation, they settled on eleven players as the optimum number of players per team to insure enough players, but not so many that they'd be clogging the field with crashing bodies.

Think about dinner for special guests. If you were having one close personal friend for dinner, you would plan the menu and table service accordingly. If a dozen were coming, the menu would probably change, more time would be required for preparation, and your guests would be served differently. It would be a different occasion. What if a group of thirty were invited? Likely, you would change the menu. Instead of a sit down meal, you might plan a buffet or outdoor cookout. You would need more time and help preparing and cleaning up. Again, it would be a different kind of occasion.

Part of the relevance of this dinner party metaphor is that the smaller the worship gathering, the more the worship leader is a host and facilitator. The larger it is, even when still under one hundred, the more the leader is a coordinator or conductor. The size of the congregation calls for different leadership gifts and styles. The person who is skillful at drawing out and facilitating a group of fifteen might be very awkward and inhibited if the size of the group were quadrupled. The reverse is also true. In the process of discerning gifts for ministry, part of the discernment ought to be identifying appropriate gifts for working with particular numbers.

Gertrude Stein said a rose is a rose is a rose, but a worship service is not a worship service if the numbers change. This book discusses worship with fewer than one hundred worshipers, but that's not precise enough. If yours is a house church of a dozen, your worship should be quite different than if there are usually forty. Your worship will be even more different if eighty-five are present. This dynamic is routinely ignored in resources or books about the theory, theology, and practice of worship.

One difference will be the physical arrangements. A dozen or so would probably prefer comfortable chairs in a home living room or church parlor. Two dozen might prefer the church chapel. Four dozen or more will expect to be in the sanctuary, if it's not too large. The appropriateness, configuration, and arrangement in the worship room make all the difference between feeling at home and feeling out of place.

There are two foci in worship. One is the offering of praise and gratitude to God. The degree of formality that seems appropriate and desired changes with the numbers. The more worshipers there are, the more likely a set liturgy will be effective. With fewer people, praise and gratitude can be expressed with more intimacy, spontaneity, and specificity. More worshipers will feel uninhibited in offering extemporaneous prayers of gratitude or expressing tentative feelings. In a small group, the leader can encourage more depth of participation and will need to be prepared to respond to that depth. Each time I've collected and prayed words of thanksgiving that had been jotted on slips of paper, the composite prayer has been wonderful.

The second foci in worship is the spiritual nurture of the people that leads them toward more faithful living. Here the need to adapt to the size of the group will be even more pronounced. The fewer people present, the more spontaneous they are willing to be. The more there are, the more structured they will expect to be. The kind and amount of music may be different. A guitar may work better with fewer and a piano or organ when there are more. The fewer there, the more comfortable they will be in taking turns reading scripture around the circle and giving personal responses to it.

A smaller number frees you for more variety in proclaiming the Word or preaching. When I lived in New England, I often attended worship at the Weston Priory, a Benedictine monastery in Weston, Vermont. Between twelve and fifteen brothers were always in their worship circle. At the point in the liturgy when larger, more conventional churches would have a homily or sermon, they would reflect communally on the scripture of the day. They related their comments to what had been said before and connected the text to their life in community and the world. They more than accomplished what one would expect in a sermon. They had the benefit of the collective wisdom of the group rather than one designated preacher. Rather than being passive listeners, they energetically engaged the text and one another. If there were four times as many, this style of preaching would not be as effective or inclusive. The fewer the worshipers, the more spontaneity and specificity is possible as people engage and relate to the Word.

In the offering, praying, responses, and the sacraments, a church can be more personal, more specific, more flexible, and more immediate when there are fewer worshipers. In a course I taught in small church ministry, I led a complete worship service designed for the eighteen people. In place of a conventional offering, I told the story of a World Council of Churches worship service in which worshipers were asked to bring an offering symbolic of themselves to offer God. An African woman, carrying her baby, came forward, put the offering plate on the floor, stood in it, and said, "I offer my self, my baby, all that I have to God." Then I placed a large platter on the floor and invited the class members to come, stand on the platter, and offer God their particular gifts for ministry. This offering touched us all deeply. But it could not have worked with a much larger group, where sheer numbers would have extended the offering time to twenty minutes or more.

When it's time to offer joys and concerns and pray, people in smaller groups are more likely to share voiced concerns. They might stand in a prayer circle. With fewer people, more will pray orally. They might hold or lay hands on the person being prayed for. The fewer the numbers, the lengthier this part of worship may be. The fewer there are, the easier it is for the whole congregation to gather around the baptismal font or the communion table. These sacramental occasions may be informal and less orderly but far more personal and powerful.

Smaller churches often feel they aren't large enough to do church right. When helped to discover that they have just the right number to worship with profound meaning and that there are advantages to their size, their whole approach to worship and the church itself will be transformed.

Questions:

1. What size-related alternatives can you think of for each part of your customary worship?
2. How do you already find yourself adapting to the number who are present? Are you more informal, more interactive if fewer are there and more formal, following the order more carefully when more are present? How?
3. Develop some strategies for keeping the nature of your worship small if or when your numbers grow.

Suggestion:

Ask a group to help you imagine how each piece of your worship could or should be designed differently if there were half as many or twice as many people present.

PRACTICE #2: The Order of Worship Matters

> Those who design worship, <u>like other artists</u>, need to think about what it is they want to communicate to the people in the seats, what experience they want them to have, what part of their being they would like to touch, what realization or transformation they hope will take place so that, by the end of this activity, people will not be merely an hour older [underlining added].[2]

Pragmatically, the order of worship matters to the effectiveness of worship. Theologically, the order of worship matters to the faithfulness of worship. Spiritually, the order of worship matters to the people's hearts and minds. Ecclesiologically, the order of worship matters to the well being of the congregation. Missionally, the order of worship matters to how transformational the church is in God's world. Artistically, the order of worship contributes to the experience of worship in the same way that the paint Van Gogh put on the canvas contributes to the experience the viewer has with his art. Those who plan worship are artist and architect, rather than technician or arranger.

I generally put as much time and effort into planning the order of worship and the bulletin as I put into the sermon. The result is not an inadequate sermon, but a worship service that is a total, integrated experience. The result is a worship experience that has the same intentional progression as a carefully crafted piece of music. A well planned and conducted order of worship can compensate for other limitations in a pastor's ministry. A poorly planned order of worship is a limiting handicap to all the rest that a church is meant to be.

I've attended worship services most of the Sundays of my fifty-eight years. In many of the services I've experienced, there has been more disorder than order, more meandering that progression, more diversions than a finely focused whole. Whether the church is high church Episcopalian or evangelical Baptist, ultra-liberal or ultra-conservative, African American or Anglo American, its worship should have the same, essential three part progression—preparing, hearing, and responding.

How do bulletins contribute to the worship experience? They receive mixed reviews. Some say they're less important in smaller churches. Some say they are more of a hindrance than a help. They can be either. A poorly prepared, poorly formatted bulletin, full of typos and bad grammar, too wordy and confusing to use, with little helpful material, is more of a distraction than a help and a waste of the preparer's time and the user's attention.

A creative, well-done, thought-provoking bulletin, on the other hand, provides immediate communication with the visitor or guest. Like a menu in a fine restaurant or a playbill at the theater, it can pique the user's interest and introduce the worshiper to what's coming. It can be a meditation guide for the time before worship and for use during the week. It's the script for the drama of worship. When a carefully worded, clearly formatted, easily read script is available for all worshipers, they are more likely to participate fully and harmoniously A compassionate church will use a photocopier that enlarges to produce large print bulletins for young or visually impaired readers. While some people are oral learners and easily receive input through their ears, others of us are visual learners and can't assimilate ideas without seeing them. A printed order allows for the communication of more ideas and content than if the leader is restricted to oral communication.

A well-crafted bulletin is one of the most effective ways for a church to market itself and inform its members. We live in a print culture and all of us judge the quality of a product by the quality of its printed materials. Today, almost every pastor and or church has access to a computer for word processing and a photocopier for producing printed material. A well-executed bulletin is time and money well spent.

Back in 1971, when I became the two-day-a-week pastor of the tiny Warwick church, their order of worship was a half page glued to the inside cover of the old hymnal. One of my first acts was to get permission from the local three-room school to use their ditto machine or spirit duplicator to create a timely, interesting order of worship. Back then, that one page (front and back) purple type bulletin with the hand done or traced graphic in the top corner was evidence that the quality of worship at the Metcalf Memorial Chapel was improving. Later my wife gave me a used spirit duplicator for Christmas. After a couple of more years, I made friends with the new (and only) lawyer in town who let me use his newfangled photocopier.

Let's walk through the San Rafael bulletin. It used to have a sketch of the church building on the cover. That was a mistake. First, the church is a people, not a building. Second, everyone already knows what the building looks like and it doesn't look much different than other churches. Third, the bulletin looked the same every week, subliminally suggesting that our worship probably wouldn't be much different either. Fourth, we had wasted a page that could have been used to capture attention, stimulate imagination, entertain children (as well as adults), and communicate the truth of our faith and the theme for the day.

Each week I search two books of calligraphic scripture quotations, two books of fine pen and ink drawings of biblical stories, and two bulging files of clippings of black and white art to produce an attractive cover that addresses the theme of the day or the season of the church year. Occasionally, a relevant cartoon or piece of art from one of our children is used. The cover gets the worshiper's attention, points to what will soon be happening, and communicates that what's inside may also be of interest and importance.

Open the bulletin. At the top left is a block of information including the name of the church, date, church season. There's the name of the pastor, music director, and lay leader, and phone numbers and e-mail addresses. The last line in the heading is a notation that "The Whole Congregation" are the church's ministers. Then, in bold black print, there is a warm word of welcome to visitors and members, thanking them for attending, naming the intent for this worship, providing directions about when we stand, and reminding them that large print bulletins are available. Finally there is a thoughtful quotation to pique interest and suggest a theme for our time together.

The bulk of the bulletin is the order of worship, which is always laid out in three bold print sections or acts: *We Prepare* (to worship in God's presence), *We Hear* (God's Word in scripture, music, and preached word), and *We Respond* (with the prayers, gifts of our lives, and commitment to discipleship). That's the essential worship progression for any worship experience. Without preparation we are going to be distracted, half-hearted, and separated from God and ourselves which will make our attempts at worship fatally flawed. Without devoting time to hearing what God is seeking to communicate to us, we will only be celebrating ourselves and hearing what we already know and prefer to believe. Without seizing the opportunity to respond, we will be hoarding the Good News, hiding our gifts, and consigning ourselves to life as it has been rather than as it is meant to be.

Below is the order of worship that's still evolving, yet which I've used for thirty years. It's probably different than yours and may not be any more faithful and effective than your church's, but it's carefully conceived, works well in a small congregation, progresses from preparing to hearing to responding, gives worth to God, enables our worship to be the work of the people, makes disciples, and furthers the ministry and mission of our church. This is the basic structure for our worship. In the Worship Resources section at the back of this book, you will find an example of this order with content and interpretation that was provided on a Sunday when the theme of our worship was "worship." For the purposes of this book, there is a ✝ following each of the components in which the congregation is invited to participate beyond watching and listening. The ★ indicates where those who are able are invited to stand.

We Prepare (Act I)

Lighting of the Candles

Prelude

Welcome and Announcements ✝

   ★ Community Building (people are invited to move and greet one another) ✝

   ★ Choral Introit

   ★ Call to Worship ✝

   ★ Hymn for Gathering ✝

Unison Prayer of Confession ✝

Silent Prayers of Confession ✝

Lord's Prayer ✝

   ★ Assurance of Grace ✝

   ★ Hymn of Grace ✝

We Hear (Act II)

Ministry with Children ✝

Anthem

Hearing the Biblical Word (✝ sometimes congregation participates)

   ★ Sermon Hymn ✝

Sermon (✝ sometimes congregation participates)

We Respond (Act III)

Affirmation ✝ (a prayer, statement of faith, reading, hymn, etc.)

Time of Intercession and Prayer

  Joys and Concerns of our Community ✝

  Invitation to Prayer ✝ (two sentence response)

  Silent Prayers ✝

  Pastoral Prayer (could be a bidding prayer or sentence prayers involving congregation)

  Prayer Response ✝ (Sung by congregation)

  Offering of Gifts ✝

  Offertory (uses gifts of various musically talented people)

  * Doxology ✝

      The first Sunday of the month, a Lord's Supper liturgy begins here which includes:

      * Responsive Invitation to Our Family Table ✝

      * Passing of the Peace and Coming to the Family Table ✝

      * Communion Song ✝

      * Words of Institution and Prayer

      * Bread and Cup Carried around the Circle ✝

      * Unison Prayer of Thanksgiving ✝

      * Singing of Shalom ✝

      * Commission

      * Postlude

  * Hymn of Service ✝

  * Commission ✝

  * Passing of the Peace ✝

  * Postlude

This order is the active work of our people. On Sundays when worship does not include the Lord's Supper, the congregation participates beyond listening and watching in all but five to seven of the thirty-one separate components (depending on whether they're involved in scripture or sermon). Listening and watching comprises less than half the service.

There's a natural rhythm and progression to this order. People arrive as individuals, many feeling beaten and battered by the world. They interconnect as a community of faith and offer themselves to God just as they are. They are again promised the graces of God and return praises to the gracious One who has given and sustained their lives. They hear God's demanding and promising Word and respond with prayers and offerings and promises. They leave as refreshed and transformed disciples, ready for another week in a tough world. This basic order has provided meaningful worship for thirty years in congregations ranging from fifteen to one hundred plus (on Easter), and from a small town, blue collar congregation to an urban, highly educated one. It allows for quiet introspection and communal participation, variety, creativity, flexibility, and reassuring predictability. This is a template the reader may choose to adapt for her or his own context.

Following the order, there is a statement of our congregation's openness to any and all of God's people, news and announcements about the life and activities of our congregation, an occasional song or hymn insert for music not in our hymnal, an informative flyer or brochure, and maybe a relevant cartoon or quotation. Few bulletins are left in the pews or recycling box, which means most bulletins go home as meditation resources, reminders for the home bulletin board, or to be shared with a friend or neighbor.

Those of you who design and conduct your congregation's worship are God's artists and architects. How thoughtfully, appropriately, and creatively you do your job will determine whether you've created a masterpiece that transforms lives or the equivalent of ecclesiastical junk mail. The order of worship matters a lot!

Questions:

1. How would you describe and assess the order of worship you're used to?
2. How would you compare and contrast the order of worship in your church with the one described here? What is the meaning of the differences?

Suggestion:

Invite your people to complete the worship survey at the back of the book and discuss it with them. The results will provide clues and suggestions for strengthening your order of worship.

PRACTICE #3: Worship the God Who Loves the Remnant, the Jesus Who Turns Water into Wine, and the Spirit Who Refreshes and Transforms Us

Christian liturgy is Trinitarian. God, the creative one, is the object of Christian worship. Christ, the redemptive one, is the focus. The Holy Spirit is the animating force[3]

The implication of Benjamin Griffin's quotation is that Christian worship, as it reflects the God it worships, should be creative, redemptive, and focused. In the book *Alice in Wonderland*, it's suggested that if you don't know where you're going, you'll end up somewhere else. The same logic would hold that if you don't know the particular, relevant nature of the God you are worshiping, you will worship someone else. Any church, and in our case smaller churches, will be formed and impacted by the particular aspects of God that are prevailing and dominant in their worship. A smaller church should worship the God that is manifested in the particular divine qualities that are most relevant to its particular nature, need, and opportunity.

This principle is especially attuned to smaller churches who, like comedian Rodney Dangerfield, get no respect. In the chapter titled "A Small Theology" in *The Big Small Church Book*, I suggest that a thorough examination of biblical theology supports the conviction that God has a bias for smallness. This may rankle those who don't fit the small category, in the same the way liberation theology's thesis that God has a preferential option for the poor rankles many who are not poor.

Nevertheless, I believe an objective reading of the Bible, from Genesis through the epistles, supports the thesis that God is biased—on behalf of the poor, the dispossessed, the disadvantaged, the righteous, the faithful, the young . . . and the small. (See the whole chapter from *The Big Small Church* Book for a complete presentation of this idea.) In Genesis alone, God chose to begin again three times with smaller communities—the Noah story, the tower of Babel story, and the story of the division of Israel into twelve tribes.

The history of Israel is a cyclic saga of God's people growing large and prosperous, then unfaithful and self-destructive, with a small, faithful remnant emerging—only to repeat the tragic cycle. Remember Deuteronomy 7:7–8: "It was not because you were more numerous than any other people that the Lord set his heart on you and chose you—for you were the fewest of all peoples. It was because the Lord loved you . . . ." And Zechariah 4:6, 10: "'Not by might, nor by power, but by my spirit,' says the Lord of hosts. . . . For whoever has despised the day of small things shall rejoice." As a result of their smallness, Israel exhibited qualities of dependence and devotion which qualified her to be God's chosen people. The scriptures illustrate that the small, lacking other alternatives, must rely more on God's grace than their own clout.

The Old Testament, and especially the prophets, speak repeatedly and lovingly of and to the remnant who remained faithful when most of their peers pursued other gods. These remnant texts warrant repeated and creative preaching in smaller churches struggling to be faithful and effective in a bigger-is-better-world. The concordance offers a wide range of provocative and useful remnant texts. Following are snippets from four of them:

- Genesis 45:7———Joseph speaks: "God sent me before you to preserve for you a remnant on earth, and to keep alive for you many survivors." This could be an encouraging ordination or installation text.
- 2 Kings 19:30–31———"The surviving remnant of the house of Judah shall again take root downward, and bear fruit upward; for from Jerusalem a remnant shall go out, and from Mount Zion a band of survivors. The zeal of the Lord of hosts will do this." It would be good for all of our churches to know that they are meant to be both rooted in their biblical tradition and fruit bearing in mission, and that their God is zealously seeking their survival and faithfulness.
- Romans 11:5———"So too at the present time there is a remnant, chosen by grace." How empowering it is to believe that our smaller church is a chosen people, through the grace of God.
- Jeremiah 31:7–8———"For thus says the Lord: Sing aloud with gladness . . . and say, 'Save, O Lord, your people, the remnant of Israel.' See, I am going to bring them from the land of the north, and gather them from the farthest parts of the earth, among them the blind and the lame, those with child and those in labor, together; *a great company* . . . [italics mine]." This is the most promising remnant passage. Why does God make a great company out of those of whom the world thinks the least? If this is a great company, your church must have the potential to be one also!

In the household of God, those with the greatest handicaps and those lowest on the totem pole of power and prestige seem to surface as the great company. Churches that believe these passages and worship this remnant-loving God can never excuse themselves as too little, too poor, or too insignificant.

God has far more qualities than we readily utilize in worship, so we have to decide which attributes of God ring most true and which best speak to us of the God who is seeking us out. Smaller churches can be enriched and strengthened by researching and worshiping the remnant-loving God. But that's just the beginning of God.

How do we think of and worship Jesus, the Christ? There are many adjectives and metaphors from which to choose. I propose worshiping the Jesus who turned water to wine. What are more common than water and smaller churches? Water gets little respect except in times of drought, flood, and contamination. Smaller churches hardly ever get respect except when they do something extraordinary; however, turning plain old water to wine might qualify. From Matthew through John, Jesus perpetually did the unexpected—changing water to wine, consorting with the underclass, breaking the normative rules of righteousness, loving his enemies, and not running from Jerusalem in the end. A smaller church that pays close and imaginative attention to this Jesus just might start acting like him. Seriously worshiping this redemptive Christ might give them a vision of being water to wine-ers.

However, giving worth to the God who particularly loved communities like yours and praying to a Jesus who only accomplished remarkable things will only produce a people full of admiration and hope . . . unless there's a transforming spirit moving among them. And where does a church find such a spirit? It will find it by remembering to worship the rest of God—the Holy Spirit who refreshes, sustains, transforms, and animates. This is the same Spirit who turned a dispirited band of nostalgic Jesus lovers at Pentecost into rabid, cross-cultural, fire-breathing evangelicals who in one day created something like one hundred house churches of thirty or so each. (I'm extrapolating from Acts 2:41–47 where we read that three thousand were converted by Peter's preaching and within days they were divided into house church fellowshiping communities of probably two to four dozen each.)

How many and in what ways could such a multifaceted God be imaged in your worship? Start with the worship space itself. What kind of God is symbolized there? How could a God who particularly loves the least of these, a Christ who did nothing but the unexpected, and a Spirit who is fully immanent and energizing be represented?

How many different qualities and images of God are in our worshiping and praying vocabulary? Perhaps we could vastly expand this vocabulary, with a concentration on the images that match our people's need. The language of our liturgies is a wonderful place for our understanding of God to be stretched, enriched, and made more incarnational. Preaching that sharpens, concretizes, and particularizes the God we approach in worship will strengthen the worshipers.

Sacramental acts are wonderful opportunities for fleshing out our understanding of God. The totality of God is accessible in these dramatic acts, waiting to be made real. Baptisms, weddings, and death rituals are opportunities to expand people's understanding of God. The people who are there, waiting to be influenced, are often people you won't see any other time. Your people will start doing amazing things when you help them discover the complete God who loves them for who they are as much as for what they do.

Questions:

1. When you carefully examine your worship service, what characteristics of God are most prevalent in your worship?
2. To whom in particular do you pray? Is your God more than these names and attributes convey?

Suggestions:

1. Preach a series or have an after worship forum or series of forums on the names we call God. Start an open-ended, public list of your church's vocabulary for God.
2. Enlist a couple or more of your wordsmiths to write some fresh and real liturgical pieces—calls to worship, confessions, prayers of thanksgiving, communion prayers.

PRACTICE #4: Design Worship as the Work of the People and the Fruit of Their Gifts

If liturgy is the "public work of the whole people of God" and if each member of the church contributes to this effort according to the gift received, the style of liturgy will be determined, to some extent, by the gifts available to a particular liturgical assembly.[4]

Michelangelo was seen pushing a huge piece of marble down the road. A neighbor called to the sculptor and asked why he was working so hard to move the huge rock. Michelangelo stopped to wipe his brow and answered: "Because there's an angel in this rock that wants to come out."[5]

What have we established so far? Worship is giving worth to God. The only way to give that worth is with the gifts at our disposal. Liturgy is the framework or structure of worship and a venue in which our gifts are exercised. The word liturgy literally means the work of the people. Christian Worship is not private meditation but the sacred act of a community of the faithful. It is not a performance by a few, but a participatory act of the whole community. We participate through the people's gifts of time, talent, and treasure. In its essence, every gathering of worship is a Christmas morning around the tree when the family gives and receives gifts from one another in the name of the Christ.

In Warwick, it was Irene Boyd accompanying the organ with her cello, Clyde's communion table, Rotha's flowers, Judy's warm hug, Marge's "Amazing Grace," and Liz's hot cross buns. In Shrewsbury, it was Connie's banner, Judith's amazing voice, the Church Mouse Choir, Red and Dick handing out the bulletins, and Karleen who brought the developmentally disabled into our presence. In Emmetsburg, it was the music of the Johnson family, Doc Marks who greeted each person with a smile and a bulletin, Angie gathering the kids, Judy's clown service, and Winifred playing an offertory. In San Rafael, it's Bob Smith welcoming each worshiper, Tom's extraordinary musical versatility and Chuck's fiddling, Luise doing more things than we know about, Caryl's stories for children, Jean's floral arrangements, Bob's Easter flower cross, a long list of lay readers, and everyone who helped rebuild our sanctuary. The gift-bearing people of every church make their worship far richer and more organic.

Our smaller churches don't have spellbinding preachers like William Sloane Coffin Jr., choirs like the Mormon Tabernacle Choir, sanctuaries like St. Patrick's Cathedral, and hoards of seekers like Willow Creek. And we're probably not going to. But we can have authentic Christian worship that sustains and transforms lives and gives people the assurance that they're able and irreplaceable.

The Apostle Paul reminded almost every church he wrote to that each and every person in the fellowship has been given spiritual gifts for the good of the whole. This universal truth is still true. Every worship service is a dress rehearsal in which the cast that is the church acts their part and does their very best to make sure the play works as the playwright God intended. Dietrich Bonhoeffer, who wrote *Life Together*, the classic guidebook for Christian community, wrote:

> In a Christian community everything depends upon whether each individual is an indispensable link in a chain. Only when even the smallest link is securely interlocked is the chain unbreakable. A community which allows unemployed members to exist within it will perish because of them. It will be well, therefore, if every member receives a definite task to perform for the community, that *he may know in hours of doubt that he, too, is not useless and unusable* [Italics mine].[6]

Bonhoeffer's quotation changes the equation. The principle goals are more than getting people to attend by giving them a job and ways to participate in worship. These may be reasons enough, but the goal is more:

- Authentic Christian worship is the work of all the people—short and simple.
- Authentic Christian worship is a workshop in which all the people are encouraged and supported in naming their spiritual gifts and developing them as gifts for God and God's people, as well as their own sense of self-fulfillment.
- Authentic Christian worship provides the precious opportunity in which those now employed in the community know deep in their heart that they are not useless and unusable. Bonhoeffer is clear that at its deepest core, Christian worship is both a gift to God as well as a gift to the people themselves.

So how do we make worship more the work of the people and the fruit of their gifts? First, *Identify the Gifted.* Every person who comes through the door, even those painfully shy or feeling unworthy, fit Bonhoeffer's claim that each is an indispensable link in the chain. We probably know who sings beautifully, has a fine reading voice, or is always dependably present. But beyond these folks, in smaller churches we can name virtually every person and find ways to employ that person as a gift to God and to the person, her or himself. In San Rafael, you don't have to be there long before being invited to invest yourself. A recent serious visitor (who had been away from any church for a long time) helped preach a third of the sermon on her fourth Sunday with us. That sermon was preached by three of our newer and younger people and the theme was "The Ministry of My Life."

What can each of the elderly and the children do? Lucile, our frail matriarch, looks forward to helping produce our newsletter. Mallory played the offertory six weeks after beginning piano lessons. Churches that make room for the gifts of children in their worship will attract families. In Emmetsburg we had two emotionally fragile women who blessed our worship by sharing their piano playing gifts. I operate on the assumption that from greeting at the door to bringing garden flowers to singing to preaching to assisting with the sacraments, every worshiper has a gift to bring to the work of the people. Each week I can identify that through our worship we have helped someone not feel useless and unusable.

Second, *Equip the Gifted.* Part of our gift to the gifted is the expectation that they will share their gift with all the excellence they can muster. It's not good enough to get up and mumble through the scripture when—with some orientation and practice—the person can communicate God's Word effectively to those who need to hear it. In the resource section at the end of this book is the list of guidelines we give people before they greet, read, or tell a children's story. This past year we established a Liturgists Guild—nine people with whom I met, oriented, and worked through the month they helped lead worship. A friend of mine in Vermont started a Preaching Academy in his little church. He worked intensively with a handful of lay leaders, taught them about sermon preparation and delivery, encouraged them to preach in their own church, and then found them opportunities to preach in small neighboring churches. The goal is not to assemble a rag-tag assortment of people to merely fill slots. Rather, we want to build a gifted, equipped cadre of leaders who lead the rest of the people of God in the work of worship.

Third, turn them loose to *Utilize Their Gifts*. One doesn't train a horse and then never ride it. The level of interest and expectation rises when people come to worship wanting to see who's doing what this Sunday. The more folks are involved in worship, the more they will want to be involved, and the easier it will be for the new and the shy to take a turn. I remember Shelly, a young housewife in Warwick, who discovered through the church that she was a talented actress and a person of many gifts. Smaller churches at their best are laboratories where experiments are hatched, miracles of discovery happen, and gifts are grown to fruition.

Participating in the work of the people involves far more than providing public leadership. Some people have those gifts and some do not. There are other equally important gifts needed and represented. Writers can write pieces of the liturgy, bakers can bake communion bread, gardeners can bring flowers from their gardens, interior decorators can decorate, seamstresses can make stoles and robes, pray-ers can pray fervently that the Spirit of God will be felt, builders can build, hosts and extroverts can greet and meet, actors can act, musicians can make music. When imagination is employed, there's room for almost every gift in the liturgical work of the people.

Every church is different. Every church has a wildly different cast of characters and array of resident gifts. In addition to identifying the tasks that need fulfilling, it's at least as important and more exciting to survey and identify the apparent and latent gifts represented and then ratchet up your own creativity to see how those gifts can be used in the liturgical work of the people. Here's a brainstormed roster of some of the possibilities that might emerge in the unlikeliest places:

- A kazoo band
- A sanctuary displaying the creations of resident artists
- A drama group writing and acting the call to worship on a regular basis
- An extended prelude or postlude by the musical prodigy
- A gifted song leader leading all the hymns

- A techno-wizard creating a high tech audio and/or video sanctuary
- A wine maker making the communion wine
- A skilled Bible study leader leading fifteen minute Bible studies in worship
- Resident artisans crafting communionware, the cross, font, and table (I know a potter who made individual communion cups for all the members of her little church!)
- Dancers dancing, clowns clowning, comedians cracking frozen faces

Is there any genuine gift not usable in the liturgical work of the people? Can't you imagine God visiting with St. Peter on a Sunday afternoon:

God: Did you see who preached at_____?
Peter: Yeah, and did you hear that gospel blues piece that Bessie sang at_____? It knocked their socks off!"
God: And how about the hug from that six-year-old that brought hope to the chemotherapy patient at (the reader's church)?

At each of our churches there are as many beautiful angels waiting to be liberated from rocks as there are people worshiping. How do I know? The Bible tells me so.

Questions:

1. How many people and what percentage of the worshipers present had a specific task to perform last Sunday at your church?
2. What would have to change in order for your worship to become even more of a work of more of the people?

Suggestions:

1. Hold a conversation with one or more groups in your church, focusing on Bonhoeffer's statement and its relevance for your congregation.
2. List every worshiper you regularly see and note beside each name what potential gift that person brings to your liturgical life.
3. Start a lay leaders academy and see what happens.

PRACTICE #5: Center Smaller Church
Worship on People, Not Tasks

> While the small church is not always beautiful, it is enough. Small is enough. It is enough for keeping on. It is enough for faithfulness. It takes two or three, Jesus said. Most small churches have at least a dozen or two. Small is enough for holding lives and families together and for making a contribution to a community. It is enough for breaking bread and sharing wine, for wrestling with the scriptures, for calling one another to new life. It is enough for praying, for following Jesus. What else do we need?[7]

One Sunday morning, after several years in Warwick, I was more prepared and focused than normal before worship. Sitting facing our congregation, I had time and presence of mind enough to concentrate on each of the forty plus people. I realized that not only did I know every person there, I knew more than that. Looking from face to face, I realized that I knew at least one significant thing going on in the life of each person. I knew who was unemployed, who had recently celebrated an anniversary, who was experiencing family stress, who was involved in a community issue, who had illness in the family, who was expecting a baby. I knew whose smile was reflecting an inner joy and whose was masking pain and anxiety. I knew who was in a fertile period in their lives and who was stuck in an unhealthy mental, physical, or spiritual place. I knew what each needed from their community of faith. That cumulative knowledge shaped and deepened my ministry among these people. Now I am more intentional about knowing the people in each church at this level.

That awareness meant I was not convening an institutional gathering or calling strangers to worship. Rather, I would soon be inviting people I cared about, people whose hopes and fears needed to be addressed in our worship, to come with me into the loving presence of God. I knew that when I planned a liturgy, it was with the real lives of real people in mind, a congregation different from any other on the face of the earth. My knowledge placed upon me the responsibility of finding liturgical language that was the language of these people. I had the advantage of knowing which particular hymns were the songs of my people's soul and which was needed on a particular Sunday. I knew that when I preached, I was not casting words into unknown waters. Instead, I had the awesome responsibility of translating ancient scriptures into words and stories that could illumine the lives of these people in front of me who were hoping for revelation. I had the privilege of praying with sentiments that really were the prayers of these people. My intimate knowledge of these gave me the privilege of giving some the opportunity to offer gifts of gratitude for the blessings in their lives and others the opportunity to invest in their church as one place in their lives where they could make a difference. That to which I was privy made it possible for me to—as Jesus said—feed my sheep, not merely herd them from week to week.

A primary difference between pastoring and leading worship in smaller versus larger churches is that it's possible to intentionally do people-centered, not task or function-centered ministry. This is not to say that only people matter, or that fulfilling tasks is a dead end. Neither is true. Any well-conceived task addresses the issues of people. The problem is that if my sole focus is the task, I may miss the opportunity to touch people in my pursuit of the task. And I may make the appointed task the end rather than the means toward that higher end of impacting people's lives. In an increasingly high-tech and low-touch world, we have the opportunity of giving people at least one hour a week when they can be in relationship with their God and their neighbor in a very personal and meaningful way. This is an opportunity about which we need to be very, very intentional.

I talked with Michelle, the young new pastor of the church on Vinalhaven island in Maine. She was quite astute in defining her principle priorities as preparing and leading worship and visiting her people. That's not all she does, but that's what comes first. When I worshiped in the church she pastors, I could see the evidence of this focus. The worship she led was clearly conceived, sensitively conducted, people-centered. This kind of worship makes a difference.

Carl Dudley, writing about the power of a small church pastor, wrote: "Many pastors suggest two kinds of problems: they have overrated their power in changing the community and underrated their importance in touching the lives of people."[8] Pastors are not the only ones who overrate and underrate these aspects of ministry. The things that get financial grants, notice in denominational publications, and talked about at the pastor's roundtable are the new outreach ministry, the special educational venture, the new building project, struggles with the principalities and powers. What is seldom paid attention to is the worship that changes lives, the prayers for persons and concerns that are answered, the marriage that doesn't break up thanks to a church's ministry, the woman who makes a decision because of the sermon she heard, the man who is valued by the faith community for who he is rather than what he does, the vital mission venture that is staffed and funded. In our increasingly secular age, I believe that the cumulative time spent in worship in America is the most transforming single hour or two of the week in this society. Isn't that an amazing grace!

There are dangers in people-centered worship. Worship can be so people-centered that we forget the Host—God—who has called us to this worship time. If I only focus on the people I know are going to be present and the issues of their lives of which I'm aware, I may overlook the needs of the newcomer or visitor and I may miss those aspects of my people's lives of which I'm unaware. If I concentrate only on what is currently in my people's lives, it would be easy to forget to call them to where God wants them to be and what God wants them to do. If I only focus on my people's needs, I will probably overlook the community needs beyond the church's doorstep and the global crises crying out for attention. There's another danger. When I know my people well and love them dearly, I'm sorely tempted to tiptoe around the painful areas of their lives and the issues about which we don't see eye-to-eye. It's much easier to be prophetic to a crowd of strangers.

With these opportunities and dangers in mind, my people are in my mind and in my heart as I plan for the Sunday worship that's coming soon. As I plan worship, I find myself thinking about individuals, taking their issues into account, choosing the favorite hymn of someone in pain or with whom I've clashed, using personal knowledge as a basis for inviting someone to share in worship leadership, or using a worship issue as an excuse to call someone to see how they are. If a newcomer is secure enough to do so, I may invite that person to usher or be the lay reader as a step toward finding their place in the congregation. If someone is moving away, there will be a planned ritual to say thank you and good-bye. I will write down the names of people to speak of during the joys and concerns (to insure I don't forget them). If it will not be embarrassing or a violation of privacy, a name or two may get mentioned in the sermon in an affirming or thoughtful way. I plan our celebrations of baptism and the Lord's Supper in ways that make them people-centered and personal, as are our confirmation and new member rituals. The size of our worshiping congregation makes it possible for me to customize worship so its different from any worship any where else. It permits me to be an artist rather than a technician.

This congregation is so people-centered that I can count on someone mentioning in worship that another person who's been sick or away is back among us. Get well cards are circulated for the congregation to sign. I see people move from where they're sitting to sit with someone with whom they need to be in contact. Often, I'm in the uncomfortable position of having to monitor the time and limit the sharing of joys and concerns as people share news with one another. In addition to this being a time to request prayer, it's also a time to direct the shape of our ministry with one another. Someone may volunteer to coordinate a casserole brigade for someone coming out of the hospital. We will specifically name what it is we are praying for when someone is facing surgery, or a long recovery, or the end of life which appears to be near. This sharing time is very important to our people. A newer member rated this time a "10" on a scale of 1–5 in our recent worship survey. What gets shared in worship results in caring conversations and actions following worship and during the week. There is an intentional compulsion in this church to see that the worship hour is a person-centered hour.

As Carl Dudley understands: "When church size is measured by human relationships, the small church is the largest expression of the Christian faith!"[9]

People-centered worship that touches lives in a real way and connects one to another in a concrete manner is one of the things smaller churches do best.

Questions:

1. Are you more of a people-centered or function-centered person? What difference does that make?
2. In what ways is your worship people-centered and how is it task-centered?
3. There are tasks of ministry that any responsible church leader must attend to. How might those tasks be pursued in ways that are more people-centered?

Suggestions:

1. Go through your telephone list or look around your congregation on Sunday and see if you know everyone. If so, do you know something important that's going on in their lives? Do this with a group of care givers in your church.
2. Develop the discipline of calling one person each day, simply to say, "I was thinking about you and wondering how you are."

PRACTICE #6: Make Room for Flexibility and Spontaneity

Once upon a time the elder said to the business person, "As the fish perishes on dry land, so you perish when you get entangled in the world. The fish must return to the water and you must return to the Spirit." The business person was aghast. "Are you saying that I must give up my business and go into a monastery?" "Definitely not," the elder said. "I am telling you to hold on to your business and go into your heart."

This story speaks to me about the formal and informal, the planned and the unplanned dynamic in our worship. Each is necessary and dependent upon the other. Worship without form—the head or business side—results in worship without focus or coherence. Worship without an element of informality—the heart or spontaneous side—bores the worshiper and stifles the Spirit of God. The story recognizes the importance of both business and heart, formality and informality.

If the focus of worship is the remnant-loving God, the Jesus who turns water into wine, and the Spirit who refreshes and transforms, then worship will be authentic and pleasing to both God and worshiper if there is room within worship for response to this God. And if the response is to be genuine and pleasing, it needs to have room for spontaneous response. There should be some time and space in the worship that is not planned, choreographed, tied down, carved in stone. There needs to be time when the Spirit of God and the spirit of the people dance together, when words can be said that need to be said, when people can reach out and touch one another, when God is free to "do a new thing" (Isa. 43:19). This can't happen unless there is a measure of openness to flexibility and spontaneity.

I take very seriously the covenant of responsibility I have with our congregation and am, therefore, conscientious about trying to keep our worship close to the magic sixty-minute hour. However, our church has trouble starting on time and has even more trouble finishing on time. Our collective wisdom seems to be that some things shouldn't or can't be hurried. I've been worrying about whether the congregation thought I was breaking covenant with them when we ran overtime. So on our worship survey, I asked if it was bothersome when worship ran ten to fifteen minutes over. Only one of twenty-three respondents said it bothered them. When asked whether going fifteen to thirty minutes over would bother them, the response was evenly divided. I think their response was an affirmation that our worship experience is vital enough that time doesn't much matter—within reason. I think they were also saying don't constrain the flexibility and spontaneity of our worship. So we continue to seek a balance between business and heart.

Anglican worshipers may respond differently to this principle of flexibility and spontaneity, business and heart than Pentecostals, just as many Anglo worshipers will read it differently than Hispanics. The opportunity for spontaneity and flexibility may be in the silence or the public expression; it may be quiet or loud. But the principle is sound for all of us. Worship is not worship until there is response. And the response cannot always be scripted. Rote is not synonymous with ritual. Worship that is form with no freedom can grow stale and sterile. Worship that is all spontaneity with no structure can lead the worshiper in circles or out the door.

Size, again, is relevant. The larger the congregation, the more structured it's worship is likely to be and will need to be. The smaller it is, the more dynamic and responsive its worship can and probably should be. The more people who are present for worship, the more necessary it is to have a clearly defined and measured path to guide their journey. It will seem important to many to remain more business-like. On the other hand, the fewer people who are present, the more open they are likely to be to diversions, interruptions, and heart-felt responses.

The smaller the congregation, the easier it is to be flexible. On a hot, stifling day, a small congregation might easily choose to move out under a shade tree. In the midst of a heat spell, they could get the word on Saturday night that worship would be moved from the heat of the day to evening. On Labor Day Sunday, they could worship in an office building as part of a worship focus on vocation. On Christmas Eve, a small church could move as a group from room to room around their building enacting the Latin American La Pasada ritual. On Memorial Day Sunday or All Saints' or All Souls' Sunday, a small church could worship in their local cemetery, or hold their Easter sunrise service there.

In Warwick, we held an annual outdoor worship and picnic at Mount Grace State Park. In Emmetsburg, we held a summer worship and barbecue on an island at Five Island Lake. In San Rafael, most of our church goes on an October Saturday–Sunday family retreat sixty miles away. In San Rafael, we had a Friday–Sunday old-fashioned barn raising when much of the church worked together to build a new meeting room. The weekend ended late Sunday afternoon with the rest of the church joining us for a pot luck supper and worship in the courtyard.

In Shrewsbury, summers were special. Once we turned our morning worship into a late afternoon vespers service to take advantage of the beautiful Vermont sunsets that lit up our large west-facing windows. Then we had an evening service at the unwired Northam Church, so we could enjoy the antique gas lamps and the beautiful evening hymns we seldom got to sing. The last Sunday of July was the day of the annual Meetinghouse Rock service. For decades, religious services had been held near the top of Shrewsbury Mountain. The whole congregation and many other townspeople would drive up the mountain for this service and the picnic that followed. Smaller churches can take advantage of the opportunity to be more flexible in planning and scheduling.

The smaller a church is, the more spontaneous it can be. Once in Emmetsburg, I was away participating in a pulpit swap. Another pastor was assigned to our church. That was the day when, for some inexplicable reason, our organist was absent and our other two people who could play piano were away. What were they to do? My wife, drawing on her grade school piano lessons and a nimble index finger, played the hymns with one finger. The result was a memorable and moving worship service. She would only have done that as a spontaneous gesture. Amazing things happen in the spur of a moment, particularly when there aren't enough people to strike fear in a shy person. I still remember in Warwick when Ernestine quietly and spontaneously sang "Let Us Break Bread Together" throughout our communion service. My hunch is that the times we get goose bumps in worship is when something unplanned and Spirit-inspired happens.

It's in the surprises that the Spirit does some of its best work. Celebrate the surprises of the church year—a baby born in a stable, a cemetery brought to life, the loud cacophony of Pentecost. So how can we facilitate a flexible and spontaneous atmosphere? Don't over plan. Put those with a little flair in a position where inspiration can take over. Don't screw everything down or fill all the space with furniture. Change the environment by letting your decorators decorate the communion table or the whole sanctuary. Bring in vibrant colors. Welcome balloons and streamers for special celebrations.

The Spirit needs room to move. Encourage people to expect and welcome surprises. Allow the expression of emotion. Let children be present, participating, even leading. Resist the impulse to maintain control. To pursue excellence in worship is not the same as striving for perfection. Celebrate everything and everyone you can think of. Specialize in events, in preference to ongoing programs. Trust that God may be in or even behind the mistakes. Don't be too serious. Allow for a little fun. Laugh at yourself and others will laugh with you. Voltaire said somewhere that: "God is a comic playing to an audience that's afraid to laugh."

Larger churches have an image to maintain and many people to please. Smaller churches don't. Relax. Love God. Enjoy parties and celebrations as much as Jesus did. Give the Spirit room to move. Welcome surprises. Care for and forgive one another. Spread a little cheer. The Apostle Paul referred to himself and the faithful in his little churches as "fools for Christ" (I Cor. 4:10). Be a little less buttoned down and open to a little more foolishness. When we are, God may be more present and we may be more faithful. In the process we may all have more fun and find more inspiration.

Questions:

1. Does your church run over it's stated worship time? If so, by how much? If so, how is the extra time spent? How does the congregation feel about this?
2. What did Voltaire mean with "God is a comic playing to an audience that's afraid to laugh?" Do you agree? If so, then what?
3. What are the sources of joy in your church?

Suggestion:

Gather some people around good food and share memories of funny or unplanned things that have happened in church, times things didn't work out as planned, times when surprises happened, and people were unexpectedly moved. Ask if they'd like more times like that.

PRACTICE #7: Small Churches Want the Song They Sing to Be the Song of Their Soul

Love of my life, I am crying; I am not dying: I am dancing, dancing along in the madness; there is no sadness, only a song of the soul. And we'll sing this song; why don't you sing along?
—Chris Williamson

I'm just now beginning to recognize the truth of my original vision: we go to church in order to sing, and theology is secondary.[10]

It is no accident that congregational song in England developed in the small meetinghouses of dissenters rather than in stately medieval parish churches. . . . Their small intimate meetinghouses encouraged congregational song by making everyone feel "on stage."[11]

Almost everyone loves music of one kind or another. Most people love to sing, although not everyone sings in church. Why not? Some are like me, who were told early in life that they couldn't sing, so they stopped. Some may be so unhappy that they fear they will cry if they sing. Some may be too lazy or too distracted to try. Some are too busy analyzing the theology. Perhaps what is being sung is unfamiliar or too difficult, in an unreachable register, deadly boring, or not the style of music they enjoy.

One of the greatest joys of worship is that it can help the worshipers find and sing the song of their souls without having to sing alone. Most people feel worship needs music to have soul. Worship without music has less expression of what's deep inside, less of a sense of community, and less praise of the One who put the song in our soul.

Truth in advertising: the person writing this can barely carry a simple tune, can't read music . . . and loves singing hymns. I was smart enough to marry a woman who is musical and knows music, and I've surrounded myself, even in small churches, with church musicians willing to assist their musically challenged pastor. Thank you Ann, Karen, Marge, Doris, Bonnie, Judy, and Tom—the Pied Piper of San Rafael.

Let me tell you about these persons because they are representative of others who can be found in most churches and communities. These people helped me strengthen our worship by strengthening our use of music within worship.

In the Warwick church, Ann was a housewife who could and would play the old organ. She willingly tried any music and did her best, which was good enough. Marge was the backbone of the two person choir and the musical life of the church (my wife made it three and the choir grew rapidly from there). Marge had a gorgeous voice, was willing to use it without flaunting it, and was our choir director. (She even whistled in worship a couple times.) With my encouragement, this choir quickly expanded their repertoire and were soon singing a wide variety of music. We put together a songbook to supplement our ancient hymnal until we could afford new hymnals. Early on, we bought cheap recorders (about three dollars each) for the choir and were soon enjoying recorder anthems and offertories. The choir was the door into the church for two young men who quickly became church pillars. A few years later Karen, a professional accompanist, married one of our young men and contributed much to our music. Irene, a retired woman who lived in a little red house trailer, regularly accompanied the organ with her cello. Ann, Marge, and the choir deserve much of the credit for the transformation of worship in Warwick.

Doris was the music director and organist for our antique tracker organ in Shrewsbury. She took her choir work quite seriously and had a particular affinity for nineteenth century romantic church music. She willingly sought to add variety to our music to meet the various musical tastes in our congregation and was responsible for broadening the church's repertoire. The music Doris and the choir produced was a plus in our worship.

The four member Johnson family was the backbone of our music in Emmetsburg. Being choir director and pianist were two of the hats Judy Johnson wore in that church. Bonnie was our organist. Both were reliable and cooperative to work with. Given the rural flavor of the town and congregation and Bonnie's knowledge of country music, I wish I had thought of encouraging some music with a country flavor in our choir or church repertoire.

Tom, a teacher, artist, composer, musician, had been choir director, pianist, and organist for several years when I was called to San Rafael. He's been easy and helpful to work with. The choir is both faithful and talented. Two of the special musical gifts of this church are Bob (a basso profundo) and Chuck, who often plays his violin in worship. We have both an organ of fair quality and a concert quality grand piano which is used for over ninety percent of our accompaniment.

Many smaller churches can identify with various aspects of the music ministries in these four churches. None of the regular directors and accompanists were full-time musicians, music teachers, or directors. All were paid, but not as much as they deserved. All were people of faith who took their church work seriously. Except for the first year in Warwick, there were never less than eight nor more than twelve regular singers in any of the choirs. I wonder if this isn't the natural size of most church choirs. They sang because they loved to sing and they enjoyed the camaraderie of the choir. In each church, they were essential to the quality of worship.

Music really is the song of the soul and the prayer of the heart. It's integral in virtually every culture. Many people whistle while they work and sing in the shower. Most hum along or at least listen to recorded music often and have definite musical preferences. Many an Alzheimer patient remembers tunes and lyrics when all other memory is gone. My wife is not the only one I've heard say that they come to worship for the music as much as anything. Music is to worship what ice cream is to apple pie, and it always has been.

The Bible, from beginning to end, "trumpets" the importance of music in our relating to God. (For example, look at Ex. 15:1, 20–21; Isa. 12:5–6; Ps. 33:1–3; and Rev. 5:9.) 2 Chronicles 5:13–14 describes the extraordinary power of the music in Solomon's new temple: "It was the duty of the trumpeters and singers to make themselves heard in unison in praise and thanksgiving to the Lord, and when the song was raised in praise to the Lord . . . the house of the Lord was filled with a cloud so that the priests could not stand to minister because of the cloud; for the glory of the Lord filled the house of God."

Song was the voice of faith of our Christian ancestors. It was so important that Ignatius, bishop of Antioch, addressed the Ephesian church in musical metaphor. He wrote: "Your accord and harmonious love is a hymn to Jesus Christ. Yes, one and all, you should form yourselves into a choir, so that, in perfect harmony and taking your pitch from God, you may sing in unison and with one voice to the Father through Jesus Christ."[12]

Music in worship is much more than a warm-up act, time filler, change of pace, or performance. For many, music is a more expressive medium than speech, conveying greater depth of feeling than mere words can convey. Music is to words as poetry is to prose. Augustine said that the one who sings prays twice. This means a lot more praying happens in worship than we realize. Some people attend primarily to hear music that moves them and to sing their favorite hymns.

Did Dietrich Bonhoeffer exaggerate when he described the critical function of singing in the worship life of a faith community?

> Unison singing, difficult as it is, is less of a musical than a spiritual matter. . . . The more we sing, the more joy will we derive from it, but, above all, the more devotion and discipline and joy we put into our singing, the richer will be the blessing that will come to the whole life of the fellowship from singing together.
>
> It is the voice of the Church that is heard in singing together. It is not you that sings, it is the Church that is singing, and you, as a member of the Church, may share in its song. Thus all singing together that is right must serve to widen our spiritual horizon, make us see *our little company* as a member of the great Christian Church on earth, and help us willingly and gladly

to join our singing, be it feeble or good, to the song of the Church [italics mine].[13]

Ineffective church music handicaps the rest of worship. Even the smallest church can sing well if it chooses music it wants to sing and works to sing it well. Music that is well-selected, well done, and well placed will transform average worship into extraordinary worship and, thus, be a vehicle of God's grace.

The music chosen and used ought to reflect the makeup of the whole congregation. It ought to be music that speaks to and for the particular congregation, while at the same time stretching it. It should not be just the music the pastor, choir director, choir, or church pillars like, but music that speaks to and for all of the church's generations and musical tastes. Using music from other cultures can be a hospitable gesture to those with ties to those cultures and can help a church find unity with the Church universal. Many churches are adopting the use of praise music as a way of appealing to younger and more secular seekers. My preference is to use a variety of music without abandoning the great music of our tradition and to have worship be a cross cultural experience rather than just for one group or taste.

The way we use music in San Rafael is somewhat unconventional, yet it works well and strengthens our worship. Tom is a versatile musician, with a wide knowledge of different forms of music. He gets restless if the range of music is too limited or repetitive. Our congregation is diverse, with a variety of cultures, generations, and life styles. So our music mix is quite eclectic. Because our congregation loves music, it comprises about half our worship service. Here's how it happens:

Tom wants to know if I'm working on a particular theme for the service or in the sermon. Once I give him that information, he's off and running. He generally consults with the choir and gets their input and then draws on his own experience as a church musician, searches the church music library and his own music, and his wide knowledge of music. He often comes back with his ideas and we develop them together. We have five types of music in our worship, so he's working in all five areas: prelude and postlude music, anthems, offertory music, service music or responses, and hymns. He chooses from traditional church music, new church music, his own compositions, congregational favorites, classical music, and relevant popular music (like music from *Fiddler on the Roof*).

The prelude and postlude music may be general religious music or classical music, or it may be thematic music from a variety of sources, chosen for a particular season, mood, or theme. Last summer we had a service that was a celebration of the sea (we're near the coast and San Francisco Bay and have several sailors and lovers of the sea in the congregation). All of our hymns and other music had a nautical connection. Tom may use all Irish music around St. Patrick's Day or romantic music around Valentines Day or music from around the world on World Communion Sunday. He occasionally uses the organ for some of the prelude music because several of our people love the organ. We use the piano most of the time because he's a better pianist, we sing better when accompanied by the piano, and it's a beautiful sounding instrument. Particularly after my experience in this church, I prefer a piano over organ to accompany congregational singing, at least in a smaller church. It provides a sharper rhythmic element and does not overpower the congregation. Tom occasionally draws on the talents of young people in the congregation, visitors, and friends. Churches can use whatever instruments are represented in their congregation and culture—drums, guitars, strings, brass, rhythm instruments, or kazoos. There isn't just one holy sound. Just about anything or anyone can make a joyful noise to the Lord.

Anthem music is chosen from both church standard repertoire and new anthems in different styles. Frequently, Tom's and the choir's choice is an uncanny fit with the worship or sermon theme. Offertory music is chosen with three things in mind—appropriateness for the theme, music (sacred and secular) that our congregation enjoys, and as expressions of the gifts of our worshipers. Frequently, it is a vocal or instrumental solo. This can be a good place to involve children who are taking music lessons and feel ready to share their accomplishments.

There are four pieces of service music or response music we sing routinely: the doxology after the offering, a contemporary prayer response after the pastoral prayer, the chant "Gathered Here in the Mystery of this Hour" as we come around the communion table for communion, and "Shalom" after communion. We sing these regularly because we love them, but more importantly because they signify and communicate a profound meaning and sense of solidarity through their repeated usage. Tom plays child-friendly music when our children are coming to the front for the Ministry with Children and traveling music related to the children's story as they go out to church school.

Generally, we have four carefully chosen hymns. At least one is a well known, favorite hymn. I've surveyed our congregation's favorite hymns and often draw on this list. When someone requests a particular hymn, I honor the request as soon as possible. Usually there's a newer hymn in the mix of the four, but generally only one. I intentionally pick a variety of styles—traditional hymns of the Anglo church and our mainstream tradition, hymns from other cultures (our new United Church of Christ hymnal has a fine selection of these), new hymns, and gospel hymns that are not necessarily from our church's tradition, but representative of the traditions of some of our people. Within each service, we pick music with a mix of tempos and rhythms. When I want to try a new hymn, I consult Tom, and often the choir, to determine if it's singable and not too difficult. When we introduce a new hymn, the choir learns it first, and then we have the congregation rehearse it during the announcements. And we try to sing it a Sunday or two later, before it's forgotten. On summer Sundays, we leave one hymn slot open and invite favorite hymn requests.

I place hymns carefully in the order of worship. The opening hymn needs to unite people and get them on their feet and ready to be in God's presence. This is not the place for a new hymn. The hymn after the prayer of confession, silent prayers, and assurance of God's grace is a hymn of reassurance and promise. New hymns are most often used as the sermon hymn and are related to the theme of the worship and sermon. The last hymn is also never new and usually an action hymn intended to send people out as disciples to live their faith. There are three wonderful, recently written hymns that we recommend—"I Was There to Hear Your Borning Cry," "Bring Many Names," and "Spirit, Spirit of Gentleness." They can be found in the United Church of Christ's *New Century Hymnal* (Cleveland: The Pilgrim Press, 1995).

I use four criteria in choosing hymns. First, they must be singable and something our people will enjoy singing and find uplifting. Not all the hymns in our hymnal meet this requirement. Second, they must be what we as a church—at least most of us—believe about our faith and life, because, as Bonhoeffer, said, it's the whole Church singing. Third, they should fit the occasion—season of the year, church season, theme of the service, place in the service, or mood of the congregation. Fourth, I don't select any hymn too often (up to three times a year) for fear we will get bored with it and stop listening.

As a direct response to this approach to music, this congregation sings very well and is quite willing to sing new hymns and different kinds of hymns. For our church, the music we use is the song of our soul and our soul expresses itself quite well.

In both Warwick and San Rafael, we've done something that is a testament to what a small church can accomplish musically. In Warwick, we had a Lent-Easter custom of having the whole congregation sing Handel's "Hallelujah Chorus." During last three or four weeks of Lent, the music for this was passed out to the whole congregation at the end of worship and rehearsed. On Easter, with a guest accompanist, we ended our Easter celebration with a credible and inspiring rendition of that famous chorus. In San Rafael, the choir does the rehearsing, but the music is passed out to everyone, most people sing, and it's a fitting and stirring climax to our Easter worship.

Music in your church could be as important as it is in ours. You may have problems with which you have to grapple—a pastor who won't accommodate to the tradition and desire of the congregation, a balky director, or no director at all, a church divided in its musical tastes, an inadequate hymnal, or no one to accompany the music. Generally, any of these issues can be dealt with if your church is in agreement that music is important to your shared life if you are willing to work on a common understanding of the role of music in your worship, and if you tailor the music you use to the size and capability of your congregation. The answers to these or other problems will be unique to your situation. But there are answers, if you and your people have the resolve to work at it and seek creative or customized solutions.

In Shakespeare's *Twelfth Night*, one of the characters says, "If music be the food of love, play on!" We will, and I hope you will.

Questions:

1. What role does music play in your own life? In your faith? In your church?
2. Out of the thousands available, which two or three hymns would you like used at your memorial service? Why?

Suggestions:

1. Survey your congregation to see what their favorite hymns are. Draw on the resulting list in picking hymns for your church's worship.
2. Maintain a list of your people's favorite hymns so you can use them if you're called upon to plan a memorial service for one of them.
3. Hold a hymn sing and ice cream social. And then do it again soon.

PRACTICE #8: Smaller Churches Need to Experience the Scriptures as Their Own Story

Adam and Eve, Cain and Abel become the worshipers' contemporaries. Abraham, that noble old desert sheik, is a familiar figure to them. David's weakness and Solomon's folly, Isaiah's boldness and Jeremiah's heroism, Simon Peter's complexity and Nathaniel's simplicity are a second nature. . . . [14]

Our Hebrew ancestors were known as People of the Book. As a minority religion and culture in a hostile world, it was their affinity for their religious and cultural tradition, and for their story that had been passed down from generation to generation around tribal campfires that gave them staying power. It was their identification with The Book that enabled them to remember who they were, whose they were, and what they were called to be and do. As our culture becomes increasingly secular, people who choose to take faith seriously are going to be less in step and less sure of themselves. We, too, are a People of the Book. Only many of us don't know it or have forgotten what's in the book. Even fewer of us have any clear sense of what difference it makes to be a people of that particular book.

For several years I worked as a Christian education consultant with congregations in western Massachusetts. When I would ask their educators what kind of ministry with children they wanted, they would tell me they wanted their children to learn the Bible. When I would press them about what it was about the Bible they wanted their children to learn, they weren't quite sure or in agreement. Pretty much what they wanted was the same learning about the Bible they had received in Sunday school.

I've come to believe that it doesn't matter much if I know about the Bible or know the stories of the Bible, unless I've come to understand those stories as living stories and as my story. Those stories have made me who I am. It doesn't matter if I know the names of the patriarchs, prophets, and apostles unless I see that these—in their folly and faithfulness—are my faith ancestors. I've always been particularly proud of my namesake, King David, whom we know as a flawed, faithful, courageous shepherd, poet, and king. Until we come to see the Bible as our own family story, it's going to grow increasingly out of date, dusty, and irrelevant. As that happens, we will grow increasingly rootless and directionless. We will not be faithful disciples unless we are able to rediscover and reestablish deep and fertile roots in our family of origin, the People of the Book.

If worship is not grounded in scripture, the chances are excellent that it won't be grounded anywhere. Fewer and fewer people have had a solid Sunday School background, Bible study experience, and Bible usage at home. It may not be fair to put all the responsibility on worship to help our people become People of the Book, but for many or most, if they don't get it in worship, they are not going to get it at all. So let's do it thoughtfully and creatively.

There will be some for whom the idea of learning about the Bible will be a turn-off. Their assumption, until proven otherwise, is that the Bible is an archaic, confusing book, full of language and concepts beyond comprehension, about people and ideas that are no longer relevant. It's the job of those who take scripture seriously to transform that common perception. Through the way we demonstrate that scripture is important and in the way we use and interpret the scriptures, we can show that those historical people are no different at heart than we technological people. We can show that they exhibited the same qualities of love and hate, greed and generosity, faith and faithlessness, fear and courage that we exhibit.

Start with what people see in the sanctuary. There should be pew Bibles available for all your worshipers. (These Bibles should be in the language your people speak, which in most cases is modern English. If yours are not, find the money and buy enough *New Revised Standard Version* Bibles for all your worshipers, or some other contemporary translation.) Those who are readers will read it when they enter the sanctuary, just for something to read. (I think that's where both of our children got much of their biblical knowledge.) A pertinent Bible quotation at the top of the bulletin may begin their centering before worship. Have a very visible, large Bible that you use in worship. Perhaps a young person can carry it in at the beginning of worship, place it on the communion table or pulpit, and open it to the text of the day. The Bible can also lead your people out of the sanctuary and into the world at the end of worship. We had a seminary intern who habitually closed the Bible after reading the scripture and before she preached. I thought that was unwise symbolism. Let people see that the worship of your church and the preached word is centered in scripture.

Scripture can be the foundation for all of your worship, not just the sermon. Calls to worship, prayers of confession and thanksgiving, assurances of grace, invitations to pray, introduction of the offering, and commissions can all be taken from or built on scripture. If you're the one who plans worship for your church, you might have a Bible you use strictly for liturgical preparation. Every time you read a passage that has a potential usage in the liturgy, mark it and make an index and note it there.

There's renewed interest in singing the Psalter in worship reform. Some people think the Psalms begin and end with the 23rd Psalm. They can be helped to discover that every emotion we experience is expressed artfully in the Psalms. Some don't know that the Book of Psalms was originally a liturgical song book or that your hymnal has many hymns that quote, paraphrase, or are based on Psalms. One Psalm could be the basis for a whole service. The call to worship, prayers, one or more hymns, and the sermon could all come from one Psalm. Each summer Sunday, the congregation could be asked to skim the Psalms until someone finds the right one to call your people into worship that day. Once identified, it could be read in unison or the liturgist could line it out. (Lining out was a customary practice in colonial worship where the leader recited a line and the people recited it back with the same volume and inflection.) The United Church of Christ hymnal has a Psalter section in which the best liturgical Psalms are printed, with a refrain for the people to sing at appropriate places in the recitation of the Psalm.

One of the greatest missed opportunities in our worship is the way we use the scriptures during the time of scripture reading. There's much emphasis and advocacy for using the lectionary in worship. (The lectionary is a three-year cycle that has an Old Testament, Gospel, epistle, and Psalm often with a unifying theme, for each Sunday.) In many churches at least three of those selections are read, and the preacher bases the sermon on one or more. The intent is excellent, the discipline is admirable, the possibility of comprehensive exposure to the principle themes of the scriptures is intriguing. But my sense is that slavish usage of the lectionary can also be counter-productive. When too much scripture is read (unless the story is particularly captivating or the passage is very well introduced), a high percentage of minds drift off to somewhere else.

Recognizing that there are some risks, I often use scripture in worship differently and, for me, more creatively. As I plan worship, I usually start with the lectionary readings to discover if people can relate to what is there at this particular point in our shared life. About two-thirds of the time, the answer is "yes," and worship, or at least the sermon, grows out of one or more of the lectionary passages. Often I shorten the reading, believing that in reading scripture "less is more." I would rather inspire intense concentration on a single theme or particular passage or a conundrum than to read or cover too much. And if a listener's mind is going to stray, I'd prefer it stray within the field in which I'm working than to go way off into other fields of interest. In other words, I use a telephoto rather than wide-angle approach to scripture. One way of using all the lectionary passages is to spread them throughout the liturgy. One can be the basis for the call to worship. One can lead us into prayer. One is the basis of the sermon. Occasionally, I read a passage because I feel it's a very important or beautiful passage, even though the sermon grows out of a different passage.

The least effective way to read scripture is to announce: "The scripture for today is_____," then read it straight through (perhaps poorly) to the merciful end, and then move on as if to say, "Whew, that's over." It's more effective and productive to provide the context and background, state what's going on in the passage, suggest what to listen for in the reading, and perhaps ask an open-ended question to which you would like some responses after the reading. This introduction often includes a reference as to why this passage is critically important to the congregation at this time. (If it's not critically important and timely, why read it?) Knowing that many people cannot learn well unless they see what they're learning, I provide the page number and invite the congregation to follow the reading in their pew Bible. If the passage is short, we might read it in unison. Or we may read it responsively, alternating verses. I end the sharing of scripture with a phrase like: "In this passage is the Word of God for us today."

When I don't use the lectionary, I have a good reason for not doing so. I like to plan worship and preach thematically, so often there is a theme or particular issue in the congregation or society that begs to be addressed but the lectionary readings don't relate to it. If so, I may go elsewhere in scripture for a relevant passage, but our worship is always centered—either explicitly or implicitly—in scripture.

One way of addressing your people's needs or interests is to invite them to identify scriptures they would like explored in a sermon. Sometimes a chance encounter with a scripture leads me to a sermon and just as often a sermon idea leads me to an illuminating text. Scripture will always have more life if we have a dynamic and creative relation to it instead of a regimented or routine one.

There are many ways to communicate scripture beyond having one person reading word after word through to the end. Scripture sharing is one of the best and most creative ways to involve many members of your congregation in the ongoing work of the people. Let me count some of the ways:

- Many scripture passages include dialogue. If so, it's very effective to assign each speaker in the text to a different reader. Readers can come to the front or you can have them stand and read from their place in the congregation or they can stand in the aisles reading stereophonically around the congregation. Those who are the voice of God or Jesus can be either female or male.
- Much scripture is great drama. Faithfully transcribe the text into script form, with a narrator and a reader or actor for each part. The result will be good readers theater and a meaningful experience of scripture.
- A story that is great drama can be enacted, with or without a script, by one or more of your people. Two yards of fabric and a slit in the center for the actor's head is more than adequate for biblical dress. (Printed in the Resources section of this book on page 174 is a script for the Gideon story, a wonderful story for all smaller churches.)
- The one time I intentionally break my advice about too much scripture is Palm Sunday. Knowing that at least half of the people won't be present again until Easter morning, and believing that it's impossible to celebrate Easter until you've experienced the pathos of Maundy Thursday and the tragedy of Good Friday, we read the whole, lengthy passion story every Palm Sunday. This past year I checked with our board of ministry to see if they still wanted to do this. Their answer was a solid, "Yes." We alternate between the passion story as found in Matthew, Mark, and Luke. Usually the reading is divided among three readers—a narrator, Jesus, and the other participants in the action. The lengthy reading requires a shorter sermon, which is fine because the original story is better.
- Scripture is full of intriguing characters. If we want the congregation to understand that the Bible is their family history, then why

not have a pregnant woman in the congregation read Mary's Magnificat during Advent? A farmer could read one of the agrarian passages. The town mayor could read one of the Old Testament king stories. A child could read one of Jesus' teachings about children. Or the church treasurer or a banker or an employee of the IRS could read a tax collector story. A boater could read the Noah or Jonah story. Use your imagination.

- The scripture doesn't have to be one person reading to others. It can be a ten minute Bible study. When I do this, I hand out a typed transcript rather than use the pew and pulpit Bibles. People are more interactive and insightful with scripture if they're not reading out of holy writ. (In addition, the print can be enlarged for old and young eyes.) Have two or three open-ended questions printed at the bottom of the page and let the dialogue begin. The purpose is not to lead them to your predetermined truth, but to the emerging truth that will grow out of the collective wisdom and faithfulness of your people.

- Writers and illustrators of children's literature have created some beautiful books of Bible stories for the young and not so young. Use one of these with its refreshing language in place of or in addition to the Bible. Be sure to show the pictures.

- To encourage people to internalize the scriptures and make them their own, invite good story tellers to tell a well known story like the Prodigal Son, the Good Samaritan, the feeding of the five thousand, or David and Goliath from memory, rather than reading it to them out of the Bible.

- The scripture can be sung, if you have a composer in your midst. Or it can be danced, if you have dancers. Or it can be mimed, if you have a mime.

- We live in a visual, video culture. If you have a VCR and TV with a large enough screen, buy a copy of Zeffirelli's *Jesus of Nazareth* and show the scripture story instead of reading it.

The effective communication of scripture is worth your time and preparation. Only if you work to unleash the potential in the biblical story will it become your people's story with all the power and possibility that comes with that personalized identification. To paraphrase our pilgrim father, John Robinson, there are yet many ways for God's Word to be experienced by God's people.

Questions:

1. Which story in scripture do you think best parallels your own church's story?
2. What character in scripture is your personal patron Bible character? How have you shared this person with your people?

Suggestions:

1. Get new pew Bibles if you need them. Then use this purchase as an excuse for some remedial education about the Bible, which probably half to two-thirds of your people need.
2. Invite people to come to a living room to share favorite Bible stories and experiences with the Bible.

PRACTICE #9: The Smaller Church Preacher Is the Folk Dance Caller

To see things in the seed, that is the genius.
—Lao-tzu

Leaders are painters of the vision and architects of the journey.
—Joe Nevin, Apple Computer

Wise men [and women] talk because they have something to say; fools because they have to say something.
—Plato

It takes two to speak the truth; one to speak and another to hear.
—Henry David Thoreau

Since the very first official gathering of the Christian Church—Pentecost—preaching has been central to Christian worship. Seldom, if ever, has preaching lived up to the standard set that day in Jerusalem when the Apostle Peter preached and three thousand were baptized and created the church in response to that founding sermon of the Christian Church.

According to the literary record, preaching may have reached its low point in the mid-nineteenth century. In *Barchester Towers*, Anthony Trollope wrote this scathing indictment of preaching and preachers:

There is perhaps no greater hardship at present inflicted on people in civilized and free countries than the necessity of listening to sermons. No one but a preacher has, in these realms, the power of compelling an audience to sit silent, and be tormented. No one but a preacher can revel in platitudes, truisms, and untruisms, and yet receive, as an undisputed privilege, the same respectful demeanor as though words of impassioned eloquence, or persuasive logic fell from the lips. . . .

[The preacher] makes God's service distasteful. We are not forced into church! No: but we desire more than that. We desire not to be forced to stay away.[15]

Today's preacher can no longer compel parishioners to sit and be tormented. Some will rebel and stay away. Others may rebel and suggest the preacher find new captives.

Many preachers in smaller churches would retaliate and say that preaching in a small arena is as much a hardship. Some find it hard to take the task seriously when only twenty or forty or eighty attend. Some feel particularly vulnerable, being so close to and well known by their little flock. Being so close, you can see who's sleeping, who's frowning, or who has slipped out. Knowing your people so well, you know when they're tender, pained, or hostile. This intimate knowledge tempts some preachers to pussyfoot around sensitive subjects and others to lob potshots from the cover of the pulpit. Many smaller church preachers serve more than one church, which can make it difficult to focus one's preaching on the reality and context of each church. Or they may be bivocational pastors who struggle to have enough time and energy to do their other jobs while they care for the daily needs of the flock and prepare for their Sunday feeding. A smaller church that knows you well and is close enough to read what's behind the words can tell if its getting manna from God or prepackaged junk food. Last and certainly not least, there are few, if any, preachers in America who were specifically taught to preach to a small number of hearers. Being on either side of the pulpit can be a vexing hardship!

While the preached sermon seems like a dated anachronism to some, it is still considered the principle measure of a minister. Why else would *preacher* and *minister* be used almost interchangeably? I think we expect both too much and too little of the preached sermon. On one hand, many churches rank good preaching as the number one quality in a pastor. Personally, I place it below integrity, deep faith, pastoral care, general worship leadership, and even administration. A church with a faithful and effective pastor who preaches poorly will do better than a church with a spellbinding preacher who is a hollow person and an uncaring pastor. Churches intuitively know that a preacher will only merit following if the preacher walks her or his talk the other six days of the week.

Yet I don't think we expect enough of the preacher and sermon. Preaching is supposed to be more than merely interesting or enjoyable. It's supposed to change the hearer and, subsequently, the world. Anything less is not true preaching. One of my most embarrassing moments came in a preaching class at Hartford Seminary. As part of my Doctor of Ministry coursework, I signed up for a course in preaching. The course description in the catalogue said to bring a sermon on one of five texts to the first meeting of the course. Each text was difficult, so I picked the one from which I thought I had the best chance of producing a workable sermon. I prepared and preached the sermon for my congregation and filed it away until the intensive-week long course more than a month away. The first day of the course, I plucked the sermon from my sermon file, and drove to Hartford, arriving just before the start of the class— without having reviewed the sermon.

Professor Phil Swander, who I knew was a most demanding teacher, began the course by calling on each student to preach his or her sermon. I prayed fervently for deliverance and wasn't called upon until after lunch. By that time I'd reviewed the sermon and thought I was ready. Swallowing hard, I launched into what I was sure would establish the standard for the definitive sermon on King David and his third son, Absalom.

Two or three minutes into the sermon, the professor stopped me and began dissecting the sermon and its preacher. Foolishly, I protested: "But you didn't let me get to the good part." Before my words reached the back of the room, Professor Swander bellowed: "THE GOOD PART? IT'S <u>ALL</u> SUPPOSED TO BE GOOD!" What I'd preached wasn't good, and he was right. We each spent the next four days and nights writing, preaching, rewriting, and repreaching the same sermon in the pursuit of excellence worthy of a God-given congregation. Was it good by the end of the week? I don't know, but if it was, it was only by the grace of God . . . and Professor Swander.

We expect too much and too little of a sermon. But what is a sermon? It's far more than whatever is said or done during the segment in the bulletin called "Sermon." It's possible that some offerings we would not think to call a sermon, really are, and possible that some things called sermons, aren't. Consider these definitions and the wisdom inherent in each.

James F. White, considered by many as the authority on contemporary worship, writes, "The preacher speaks for God, from the scriptures, by the authority of the church, to the people."[16] The preacher does not speak merely for her or himself. The preacher does not preach about whatever strikes his or her fancy. The preacher does not speak without authority. The preacher is not speaking to a random collection of people, but to the church.

Ruel Howe, one of the wisest commentators on faith and the human condition in the last century, said preaching is more than transmitting ideas. "Preaching is an encounter involving not only content but relationship, not only ideas but action, not only logic but emotion, not only understanding but commitment."[17] Howe understands that preaching is far more dynamic and complex than one person lecturing others with religious words. Beyond content, ideas, logic, and understanding, preaching grows out of a relationship, leads to action, is laden with emotion, and requires commitment by both speaker and responder.

John Claypool, speaking at the Lyman Beecher Lectures on preaching, affirms that underneath and before all else, the "goal of the preacher is to reestablish a relation of trust between the human creature and the ultimate Creator."[18] Claypool reminds us that everyone in the sanctuary and everyone in the world is in a state of some level of mistrust with ultimacy. That mistrust may be played out in fear, anger, depression, or denial of faith. The preacher's fundamental task, every Sunday, with each listener, is to reestablish the state of trust so that the hearer can go on living and believing that there is meaning, purpose, and a holy calling to one's living. Without this foundation, nothing else matters.

Fred Craddock, who has literally written the textbook on preaching, believes you can't talk about preaching apart from the person of the preacher, and this person is expected to have four qualities—faith, passion, authority, and grace. It's the preacher's faith that makes the preacher believable and trustworthy. The preacher must have a passion for the truth, for the church, and for the world. Without passion the preacher won't be persuasive. The preacher must preach with authority, which is what gives one the right to speak on behalf of God, as a valid interpreter of scripture, to and for the church. In one way or another, Christian churches grant authority to those they particularly believe are called, equipped, and accepted as being worthy of interpreting divine truth for the church and world. Finally, the preacher must have grace that keeps the preacher listening, living experientially in relation to the divine, and recognizing God's serendipitous presence in her or his life and ministry. Without these qualities, one may stand up and talk god-talk, but will be a counterfeit preacher.[19]

It's easy to get caught up in the techniques and assumptions that surround preaching, but Jay Weener reminds us that, "Preaching is an art. For that reason it can never be reduced to the mastery of certain techniques which automatically produce good sermons. Though there are certain skills to be learned, preaching is not a matter of technique but of being."[20] If preaching is an art form, then there's no rigid formula or precise definition of what is or is not a sermon or how one should or should not preach.

Preaching is not an isolated action, something that can happen any time or any place. "Liturgical preaching is preaching that is done in the worship of the church. . . . Therefore all preaching, from the fact that it is preaching, is liturgical," writes Gerard Sloyan.[21] This may seem too obvious to mention, but it's too important not to. Preaching is an intrinsic component of worship, growing out of what has gone on before and leading up to what comes after. The sermon is like the dramatic action in a play that is the second act bridge of exploration in the drama that leads from the first act of anticipation to the third act of resolution. The worship liturgy is incomplete without the Word being proclaimed and the proclaimed Word is an orphan without its relationship to the liturgy.

Preaching is still more than all of this. Henri Nouwen, one of the liturgical and spiritual masters of our time, says there are two essential aspects of preaching—dialogue and availability.[22] Both are relevant and crucial to preachers in smaller churches, because both qualities can be particularly realized in such a setting. The larger the congregation, the more difficult it is to engage in dialogue and be available. By dialogue, Nouwen means the preacher's job is to preach truth that connects with the hearer's life experience. Vague abstractions and pious platitudes don't enable dialogue. In fact, they prevent it. When the congregation is smaller, there is greater possibility for a dialogue that will deepen the preacher's truth and the relevance of that truth for the hearer's life. There are real and diverse ways of facilitating real dialogue that can take place when preacher and hearer explore the Word together.

Beyond initiating a dialogue, the preacher must be available. Being available means opening our own vulnerability and humanity to back up our good words. It means a willingness to share your real self with your parishioners and a willingness to walk with them through their "valley of the shadow." St. Francis was talking about availability when he advised that we should preach the gospel and when necessary, use words.

All this wisdom and obvious truth makes preaching seem too awesome and overwhelming for any mere mortal. And it is. However, somebody has to do it. And that somebody is persons like you and me. Kathleen Norris is a small town lay preacher in South Dakota. She's also a wonderful poet and an amazingly astute lay observer of things theological. In *Amazing Grace*, she writes about her humble assessment of herself as preacher, an assessment which fits me and may fit you. She says she preaches, when she does, because someone asks her to. It's a humbling tribute when someone discerns that another has sufficient wisdom to stand in a pulpit. She says she doesn't preach because her faith is especially strong or worthy of imitation. Her experience and mine is that the responsibility of preaching is more faith building than faith demonstrating. Kathleen Norris confesses she doesn't preach because she's a model Christian. If that was a prerequisite, 99 percent of churches would not have a preacher. She admits that she doesn't preach because she thinks she's particularly good at preaching. The preacher who has concluded that he or she is a really fine preacher is probably deluded and past due for retirement. She summarizes her sense of herself as a preacher by saying: "I have to settle for doing the best I can."[23]

The wise and sensitive preacher adjusts the nature of the preaching to the size of the space, as well as the number of people present. Some preachers are more suited to one type of space and some to the other. The more cavernous the space, the more the preacher must project, exclaim, and rely on amplification, and the more assertive and explicit the preacher must be. The smaller the space, the more intimate the preacher may be, the more that can be said with the eyes, face, body, and suggestive inflection and pacing. The larger the space, the more formal the preacher may be. The smaller the space, the more an informal, conversational, and personal style will communicate. In a larger space, the preacher is restricted to a speaker-to-listener style of communication. A preacher has more alternatives for using a variety of methods and formats in a smaller space. The smaller the group, the more likely it is that they will hear and respond as a community rather than as a collection of individuals. In other words, one preaches at a couple hundred or more and to a hundred or so. One converses with seventy-five who are known pretty well. One visits with thirty or forty who are good friends. One has a heart-to-heart talk with twenty or less.

The expectations of the hearers play a role in the method of communication. In a large congregation and in what feels like a lecture situation, the hearer will expect to be spoken to in a general way. He or she will not expect to respond to or process the communication in more than a passive and internal manner. The smaller the group of listeners, the more ready the hearer is to respond. She or he will respond more quickly to humor, will be more willing to speak if a question is posed or an invitation to speak offered, and may be more likely to say, "Here am I, send me."

Until geneticists learn to clone James Forbes, Fred Craddock, or Barbara Brown Taylor, each of us will have to preach with whatever special gifts and limitations we have. Some of us can memorize, and some can't. Some are funny, and others aren't. Some are eloquent and some stutter. Some of us are poetic and some are ponderous. Some talk too fast and some talk at just the right speed. We each have to preach with the tools we've been given, maximize our strengths, compensate for our limitations, and work on using our tools as deftly as possible in practicing the craft of preaching. Then we rely on grace for the rest.

On the personal debit side, I am incapable of memorizing or even remembering all of or the order of what I want to say. My mouth can't always get all my words out distinctly before my racing mind directs it to say something else. On the credit side, I have a gift for using particularly effective combinations of words that pierce to the heart of the matter—if I can write them down first. I have a good sense of humor, a large stable of effective stories and quotations, and a wide range of subjects with which I'm familiar. I have a solid knowledge of biblical theology on one hand and our people and their world on the other.

I have a passion for the Christian faith and church, compassion for my people, and authentic sincerity and integrity.

So how do I work with my pluses and minuses in practicing the craft of preaching? The conventional wisdom is that in order to communicate more personally with the congregation, a good and effective preacher shouldn't use a manuscript. After I'd preached for years with notes, Professor Swander convinced me (and many others) that just as a good actor speaks from a carefully crafted script, a good preacher will have a carefully crafted manuscript. The issue in effective communication is not whether you have a manuscript, but how effectively you use one. So I use a carefully articulated manuscript and work to communicate as effectively as possible with it. I use words that are natural to conversation rather than to written communication.

There are other, seldom recognized virtues of manuscripts. The manuscript enables me say exactly what I want my people to hear rather than all the other stuff I might have said if I were improvising. It allows me to be more accountable for what I say. If a sermon or a funeral eulogy or wedding homily touches someone, I can provide them with a copy of what was said as quickly as I can turn on the photocopier. It also gives me more versatility in what I preach. It's easy to be lazy without a manuscript. Some preachers preach the same handful of sermons over and over again just by changing words, stories, and quotations. Finally, because I rework and revise my sermon, I can get to the point, say it well, summarize, and quit, rather than going around the barn a few extra times. In other words, I can say what I want to say in fewer minutes than my extemporaneous colleagues. With shorter sermons (ten to twelve) minutes, there's more time for the congregation's participation in the sermon time and rest of worship. I can say more that's worth hearing with ten minutes of carefully crafted, focused, coherent words than twenty minutes of rambling, repetitive wordage. When it comes to preaching, less is more.

I customize my sermons to the congregation. It's for them, about them, about the context and times in which they live, about the particular vision for ministry and mission that is finding life and shape among us. While respecting privacy and sensitivities, names may be mentioned—always lovingly, never critically. Congregations who listen to the same voice and the same approach to faith and life may grow weary and immune to the preacher after a few years. To prevent death by familiarity, I keep reading and learning and use great variety in the way I preach and how I use the sermon time. Every sermon is centered in scripture and the gospel, but like a junk ball pitcher, I have many different pitches. With apologies to Ed Linn, who taught me that a good sermon always has three points, if I preach a traditional three-point sermon, it's purely unintentional.

In thirty years of preaching in four very different congregations, I don't think I've ever been accused of being too unconventional, even though I often am. One of the reasons each of my congregations has been accepting and responsive is that they knew that I loved them dearly. Even when I've been privately unhappy with them, I've resisted the temptation to use the pulpit as a bully pulpit from which to lecture them. We should always be more understanding and tolerant with those we love and with those who love us. That goes in both directions between pulpit and pew. I believe all congregations want those four qualities that Craddock named—faith, passion, authority, and grace—in the sermons that come their way, and they want their lives to be illuminated. If the preacher does that carefully and caringly, they will embrace or at least accept whatever communication methods are used to convey faith, passion, authority, and grace.

I see both the worship leader and the preacher as the caller for the congregational folk dance, not one who performs or dances alone. With this image in mind and building on everything that's been said so far, here are a variety of ways to preach or lead the sermon part of the dance. These are not intended to be prescriptions for you, but examples to help you develop your own appropriate ways, using your own particular gifts, and the particular resources of your congregation to effectively communicate the gospel year after year with your people in your setting. (Our people can count on a fairly conventional sermon two or three times a month.):

- A traditional sermon, starting with scripture, exploring its meaning and intent, leading to what the Spirit may be calling on the congregation to do in response, with appropriate illustrations.
- A traditional sermon after the congregation starts the sermon by giving their response to the scripture or to a question or situation I've posed for them. I urge people to speak up, be brief, be respectful, and say what they want to say as their view of the truth rather than the whole truth.
- A traditional sermon before the congregation is invited to finish the sermon by responding to what they've heard or been led to think in response to what they've heard. My invitation to respond may be open-ended, or I may pose a particular question or subject. I watch the clock so as not to impinge on the other important components of our worship or my time covenant with the congregation.
- A sermon that responds directly, immediately, and personally to what is happening in the midst of the congregation—a tragic death, a critical decision, a church problem, a new initiative, a major

community issue, a shared joy. In a smaller church, the sermon can be more a piece of the business or life of the church.

- A story sermon in which a lengthy and profound story is shared as the bulk of the sermon, usually with an introduction and summarizing conclusion. ("The Rabbi's Gift" story in the conclusion to *The Big Small Church Book* is a profound sermon all by itself.)
- Once we had an artist/clergy person paint a picture as she talked about the creative process and what she was painting.
- Find the way to use the talents represented in your congregation, community, or denomination: actors who can dramatize a piece of drama, musicians who can preach through music, and so on.
- Use a community person who's in the news or at the center of an important community issue to speak. The pastor or leader can provide the biblical and theological context and insight before or after the talk.
- Swap pulpits, maybe even choir and preacher, with a neighboring pastor or rabbi.
- Occasionally, I use a book or the writings of an author to form a sermon. I preached a sermon memorializing Henri J. Nouwen, one on Annie Lamont's *Traveling Mercies*, one on the writings of Kathleen Norris, and one on cartoonist Charles Schulz (with cartoons) at the time of his death.
- Use different forms of technology to communicate illustrations the same way stories and illustrations have been used since Jesus told parables. I've used audio tape and, more often now, video tape. A videotaped commercial or segment from a program might be a launching or landing pad for a sermon. Many people in our pews are thoroughly accustomed to having the preacher preach using nothing but words; however, almost all these people go the movies and watch television and may find what they experience there more impacting and memorable than what they hear in the Sunday morning sermon. If we're serious about reaching out to unchurched folk, many of those are people who respond more readily to visual rather than oral messages. Most people will remember longer and be touched more deeply by messages that are both visual and oral. So, a half dozen times a year, I bring a fairly large-screened TV and VCR into the sanctuary. In the context of the sermon, I introduce the issue or theme of the clip and what has occurred before the particular clip or clips I'm going to show. I play up to four or five minutes of the film and then preach in relation to what they've seen. Some I've used are *Dead Poet's Society, Rudi, Babette's Feast, E. T.: The*

Extraterrestrial, Tender Mercies, Dead Man Walking, Places in the Heart, The Spitfire Grill, Romero, and *Jesus of Nazareth.* Vignettes from some of the more thoughtful television dramas and documentaries could be good sermon subject matter. The preacher might want to keep a blank videotape in the VCR so that she or he is ready to capture poignant illustrations. It would be wise to seek permission to use commercial material, and it's possible to buy a blanket license. The response to occasional use of film has been quite positive.

- A biblical or historical character can be dramatized, with the actor or preacher telling the character's story. I've done this by dramatizing Johnny Appleseed, Martin Luther, Noah, blind Bartimaeus, and Simon Peter. This is a good way to use the dramatic gifts of parishioners

- I like to invite our own lay people to preach part or all of a sermon. In every church, we have gifted people working to live their faith and make a difference in a difficult world. How better to realize the priesthood of all believers and worship as the work of the people than to invite representatives of the people to preach from their own life? Most recently, I interviewed one of our retired members who's had a remarkable life as a pastor, campus minister, social activist, and college professor. I gave him prospective questions in advance, and reserved the right to add follow-up questions.

- About once a year we have "Ask the Pastor" Sunday when people submit written questions about faith and life to which they would like me to respond.

- One summer Sunday, we had Chinese Fortune Cookie Sunday. All our worshipers found a different provocative quotation about matters of faith and life on a slip of paper in their bulletin. To form the sermon for that day, I asked volunteers to stand, read, and comment on the wisdom of their quotation. The result was highly interesting and thoughtful, and this sermon was certainly the work of the people, although my preparation for it took as long as a conventional sermon.

- Another summer Sunday, the whole worship service was focused on hymns. For the sermon, people were invited to name their favorite hymn and talk about its meaning for them. And then we sang them.

- With a different graphic or piece of art on the bulletin cover each week, sometimes the cover of the bulletin becomes an illustration in the sermon and people can be invited to comment about it.

- For several years we had a SermonWrighters group that met with me to study the text or texts for a coming Sunday and then to discern the sermon in the scripture for this church at this time. I, as the preacher, took their wisdom, added some of my own, and crafted the collective wisdom into a sermon.
- Believing that all of us are smarter than any of us, a communal Bible study can be a profound sermon. The passage is printed or provided, the leader provides the context or sets the stage and then poses provocative questions to the congregation. This encourages scripture to be taken seriously, respects the collective wisdom of the congregation, and helps people find their voice within the congregation.

It's easy to see that each of the above approaches to sermons can be especially workable and advantageous when there are fewer than one hundred worshipers. I'm relieved that I don't have to keep the attention of five hundred passive listeners in a large auditorium. Reflecting on the many strategies for preaching, the question is not "Have the people heard a traditional sermon?" but "Have they experienced the gospel intersecting with what God is intending to do through us and in our world so that we can respond liturgically and as disciples beyond the doors of the church?"

Questions:

1. How would you complete these sentences: Preaching is . . . ? A sermon is . . . ?
2. Is your understanding of preaching different than the author's? How?
3. Are there other than traditional forms of preaching you would like to use?

Suggestions:

1. Ask a group to share their recollections of their most memorable sermons.
2. If part of the task of the preacher is to scratch people where they itch, ask them to share with each other the most pressing and puzzling issues of their lives.
3. If you are comfortable asking, invite your people to complete the preaching questionnaire in the Resources section of this book.

PRACTICE #10: Worship Should Be Seasonal, Celebratory, Eventful, and Keyed to Life's Stages

For everything there is a season, and a time and purpose for
every matter under heaven;
a time to be born, and a time to die,
a time to plant, and a time to pluck up what is planted. . .
a time to mourn and a time to dance. . .
For everything there is a season,
And a time and purpose for every matter under heaven.
—Ecclesiastics 3:1–8

There is, indeed, a time for all things under heaven.
And for all the great rites of passage;
Weddings and funerals, graduations and retirements.
A time for anniversaries and reunions;
For sunrise and sundown, for moon and rain, for stars.
A time for the first breath—"ah"—and the last breath—"oh."[24]

One of the things that smaller churches are absolutely the perfect size to do is to celebrate the seasons, events, and stages of life that enrich our sacred and personal lives. One of my wife's favorite celebrations of the year is Pentecost because it can have all the surprise and delight of Christmas without all the work and cultural excess. Where I am a pastor, we celebrate many things, could celebrate more, and no one has ever said, "Why did we do that?" "That was a dumb idea," or "What a waste of time and effort." One of God's finest gifts is the seasons of our lives which we too often take for granted. The seasons are markers along the way that remind us we are not where we once were or where we will be. They are watering holes where we gather with friends to remember, celebrate, and think about things that matter. Because we celebrate them communally, they remind us about to whom we belong and where we have been together. Our celebration of the seasons, events, and stages of life can infuse the secular with sacred meaning and value.

Soon after I came to San Rafael, the church had a serendipitous celebration, actually two. My wife was having her fiftieth birthday the spring after we arrived. Because we did not yet have a circle of friends outside the church, I asked the church to help me give her a surprise party. During worship, the church's children quickly decorated our fellowship room, and after the postlude Lucinda was honored with a short and great celebration of a half-century of life.

A few days later, I raised a small personal dilemma at a meeting of our pastoral relations committee. I would soon be observing the twenty-fifth anniversary of my ordination. I commented that I wanted to observe that in some way, but that I would be embarrassed to have the church give the Rays two celebrations in the space of a month. John Starkweather saved the day by saying, "Let's celebrate what all of us were doing twenty-five years ago." It was a wonderful idea. A trip to the county library helped us discover what happened in 1969. A photo of Neil Armstrong taking the first walk on the moon was on the cover of the bulletin. The whole liturgy observed the significance of time passing. The sermon put this in a biblical and theological context. I was able to talk about what I'd learned in twenty-five years of ministry. People shared in worship about the significant events in their lives of a quarter-century ago, which gave them a sense of the course of their lives. Following worship, the church had another great celebratory party. (Partying is one of the things this church does best.)

One of the unique characteristics of both the Judeo and Christian traditions is the number and importance of seasonal celebrations in both traditions— Advent, Hanukkah, Christmas, Epiphany, Lent, Passover, Palm Sunday and Holy Week, Easter, Pentecost, Rosh Hashanah, Yom Kippur, All Saints, and All Souls Day. What is it in our religious makeup that has made us such a celebratory people? How has our celebrating led us into the new thing God is doing? The religious holidays are only beginnings to the events we might celebrate. A walk through the calendar shows cultural markers that could be invested with faithful significance—New Years; Martin Luther King's Birthday to mark the advances and challenges in racial justice; Valentine's Day; Presidents Lincoln and Washington's birthdays could be a time to celebrate our Christian relationship to our national heritage; St. Patrick's Day; Mother's Day; Memorial Day; Children's Day; Father's Day; Independence Day; Labor Day; Columbus Day (as a time to remember that almost all of us are immigrants from somewhere else and to acknowledge what happened to Native Americans in the process); All Hallows Eve (Halloween); All Saints Day; and Thanksgiving.

I've seen the church year become more prominent in the life of the church and much more creatively observed. Numerous resources are available which can be useful in creating seasonal celebrations that fit your church. Customize your celebrations to reflect the size and personality of your particular congregation and context. The seasons of the church year allow you to change the colors and appearance of your sanctuary and the mood and emphasis of your worship, so that by the end of the church year you've led your people through all the spiritual themes of the Christian faith. A family service at the beginning of or during each season can make your worship more intergenerational.

Let's walk through the year:

- ADVENT: Have an Advent-Christmas committee to help plan the season. This shares the responsibility and contributes again to worship being the work of the people. Help the committee understand that Advent is a thoughtful preparation for receiving God into our lives, not a wild celebration of that for which we're not ready. Like it or not, Advent-Christmas is a frenetic time in our society. Celebrate this season in a way that is refreshing and delightful, without being labor intensive. Encourage your people to wear blue or purple on the first Sunday or all the Sundays of Advent and have the worship leaders wear the appropriate colors. Have an Advent Workshop to prepare decorations for the sanctuary. Add new decorations each week so the season builds—greens one week, a bare tree the next, decorate the tree (perhaps during worship) the third, and poinsettias the fourth week. If you don't have one, acquire a nice crèche or manger scene, but don't put the baby Jesus in until Christmas Eve. Each week, use an Advent wreath and candles with an appropriate liturgy. We ask a different family to light it each week, asking newer families first. We've also paired a family with a single elderly person. Use more of a story emphasis and intergenerational involvement during this season. Be thoughtful about how you use music. Don't be such a purist that you cause your people to miss out on one of their greatest joys—singing favorite, meaningful carols. Every Sunday in Advent can be a special, memorable preparation for God's entry into our lives.

- CHRISTMAS: In Shrewsbury, Emmetsburg, and San Rafael, I have instituted a second, more contemplative, late Christmas Eve service to compliment our earlier family-oriented service. It's shorter, quieter, more intimate, and includes communion. It gives people a choice and allows for differences in family schedules. The color shifts to white and the congregation could be encouraged to dress in white or blue and white. For our congregations, as well as for me, our Christmas Eve services have been magical times. It's so magical that one of our young children in Shrewsbury said loudly to her mother as she headed down the aisle dressed as one of our angels, "Mommy, I don't know if I can fly!" People haven't forgotten our recent Christmas Eve La Pasada ritual in which people were greeted by Mary and Joseph when they arrived and taken to each door in our courtyard seeking hospitality. They were turned away each time until they got to the sanctuary, where they were warmly welcomed and invited in. In some congregations, a Christmas Day service is more significant than the Christmas Eve service. However your church celebrates Christmas, use your liturgy to help your church celebrate not just what God did back then, but the new thing God is doing in our lives this Christmas. Advent-Christmas is a special opportunity to reach out to and attract new folks. Work on your practices of hospitality.

- EPIPHANY: A church can celebrate the twelve days of Christmas and Epiphany and have the season all to itself after our culture forgets about Christmas on December 26th. Have a birthday party for Jesus on whatever day Epiphany falls. This season remembers Jesus' baptism, the visit of the magi, Jesus' family's flight to Egypt, and our own response to God's entry into human life. We've used Epiphany Sunday as our Stewardship Sunday when we brought our pledges to the manger (which was still in place) just as the magi brought gifts.

- LENT: Last year we prepared for Lent with an all-church Fat Tuesday party. The next night, several of us came back for a traditional, candlelight Ash Wednesday service with music, liturgy, and imposition of ashes. The liturgical color turns to purple in Lent. Some churches drape their cross in black or purple throughout Lent, while others wait to do this on Good Friday. We generally have a study group during Lent. In Warwick, we used a commercial Lenten banner kit in which a new panel was added to the banner each week of Lent with a related liturgy. Lent ends with Holy Week. Our Holy Week begins with a Palm parade of the congregation from the courtyard into the sanctuary. The reading of the Passion story is the core of this worship service. On Maundy Thursday we have a different service each year—an authentic Jewish seder, a catacomb worship such as the early church might have had, a tennebrae service, an agape meal, a foot washing service, or a drama. In San Rafael, we open the sanctuary for meditation on Good Friday and have devotional material to read, recorded music, and candles that can be lit in remembrance. In Emmetsburg, we began a round-the-clock vigil in the sanctuary from 3:00 P.M. Good Friday until 6:00 A.M. Easter morning. Everyone in the congregation was invited to sign up to sit in the sanctuary for one or more shifts. Again, devotional material, candles, and recorded music were available.

- EASTER: A church's Easter celebration might begin with a sunrise service. In San Rafael, it is an ecumenical service hosted by four congregations. In Warwick, we moved the sunrise service from place to place in town, including the cemetery. And in Emmetsburg, while the other churches had their services in their warm sanctuaries, we UCCers shivered our way across a bridge out to an island in Five Island Lake. The highlight of Easter in San Rafael is our Easter cross. In our old sanctuary, our cross was made of plain lathe. On Easter, the cross was bedecked with hundreds of flowers and was always incredibly glorious. When we rebuilt our sanctuary, one of our men built a new cross designed so that we can still decorate it with flowers. For me, the other Easter inspiration is the singing of the "Hallelujah Chorus."

- PENTECOST: On Pentecost, the liturgical color changes from white to red and the tempo increases. People are asked to wear red and most remember to do so. The symbols are fire, the dove, and wind. All it takes is a little imagination to create a memorable and Spirit-filled Pentecost. Lots of red and white helium-filled balloons, a birthday cake for the church, and a kite flying party after worship are three of many possibilities. In Warwick, we covered the green front door with bright red paper. Each worshiper was given a red crepe stole to wear.

Beyond the formal sacred and secular markers are others that could be turned into celebrations—summer and winter solstice, a Rural Life Sunday and a Blessing of the Seed Sunday, a First Fruits service in which gardeners bring the first produce of their gardens to be shared with others, a graduation Sunday for all your young people who are graduating, a Harvest Sunday, and celebrations to correspond with events that are unique to your community. For example, Emmetsburg is an Irish community, so we always had Irish prayers in our liturgy the week of St. Patrick's Day.

Then there are the celebrations keyed to the life passages of your own people. Birthdays (or at least major ones, or the birthday of your oldest or youngest person) can be celebrated. I've wanted to find the baptism dates of as many of our church folks as possible so that we could celebrate our birth into the Christian family rather than the traditional birthday observance. A church could take confirmation more seriously by having a service to honor all those who have been confirmed in your church down through the years in one grand service. I was impressed by a church in Schleswig, Iowa, that had a display of photos of every one of their confirmation classes going back almost one hundred years. People celebrating twenty-fifth or fiftieth anniversaries could be invited to have a renewal of their vows within Sunday worship. There might be a couple for whom it would be appropriate to have their wedding ceremony within the context of Sunday worship.

Some memorial services could be celebrated in Sunday worship. The first anniversary of the death of active members could be remembered in worship with a prayer or brief liturgy. The church might have an annual service of remembrance for the families and loved ones in the church who lost someone close to them by death that year. It might be healing to do this at Christmas time, a painful season for those who are grieving. Various church anniversaries can be observed.

The pastor could offer and be ready to do specialized liturgies for people— a service for those who've experienced a miscarriage or had a still birth, a service of acknowledgment for couples who are divorcing, a service welcoming an adopted child, a house blessing for those moving into a new home, a blessing of the animals service, a service of reconciliation after the resolution of a lengthy feud. Every pastor and church needs to be ready to say whether they will perform and host a service of holy union for a homosexual couple wanting to make a life-long commitment. The service I officiated at for a lesbian couple was wonderfully meaningful and healing for family members. This list is only the beginning of the possibilities. These are worth pursuing if we believe that all of life is sacred, and if we believe the Church should care about everything for which there is a season.

Emmetsburg was a community heavily dependent on agriculture. A long drought preceded my ministry there, and the farm crisis was still in effect. A blessing of the seed service, found in an old Methodist hymnal, was updated and held during our morning worship at the beginning of planting season. Sid and Bonnie, representing one of our two active farming families, brought bags of corn and soybean seed and a tub of topsoil. These were placed on the platform in the chancel. A seed blessing ritual was observed. Following up on that experience, I envisioned having an ecumenical, community-wide blessing of the seed service in which all the local farmers would be invited to come on their tractors, pulling wagons of seed for a city-wide or county-wide liturgical ritual. Unfortunately, I moved to California before this could be organized.

Perhaps it makes clergy weary to think about planning celebrations and liturgies or rituals for all these markers. First, you wouldn't be celebrating all of those every year. Second, many of them would be celebrated within Sunday worship, so there wouldn't need to be a lot of additional effort. Third, it's possible that the pastor wouldn't have to do all the planning. Fourth, this kind of emphasis in one's ministry elevates the religious leader to the unique position of chief ritual maker in our communities and society. And fifth, in my experience, it's preparation of and participation in these kinds of celebrations that I find refreshing and renewing for my ministry. Celebration of the seasons of the church year and other significant events in the lives of our people makes our worship not what we routinely do, but what we especially do, one of those things for which are known.

Questions:

1. Why do you think seasonal markers are so prominent in the life of the Judeo and Christian traditions?
2. What liturgical rituals does your church annually celebrate? Are any of these unique to your congregation? What do they mean to the life of your congregation?
3. Outside of church, what do you ritually and regularly celebrate in your own life? What value do you place on these observances?

Suggestion:

Create a new liturgical celebration in the next month or six weeks. Plan it. Do it. Assess its meaning for the people and the church.

PRACTICE #11: A House, People, and Liturgy of Prayer

> Christian liturgy is, first and last, praising, blessing, and thanking God. It is a continual speaking of God's name in gratitude and thankfulness for the self-giving of God to the world. . . . All the modes of liturgy as prayer—praise, thanksgiving, and supplication—work in relation to one another.[25]

Prayer is two way communication between God and God's people. From the human side, it can be in words carefully phrased, sighs too deep for words, or emotions responding to the presence of God's Spirit. We often act is if prayer is one-way communication—humans talking to God. Wrong! Prayer goes both ways and full circle. It involves listening, speaking, sensing, aching, exulting, coming clean, questioning, exclaiming, reassuring, praising, requesting, accepting, acting. Prayer is both intentional and unintentional communication. It's both very personal (go into your closet to pray, Jesus said) and very public.

To worship is to pray, and when two or three or more pray, they are worshiping. If prayer is communication between God and God's people, then worship is communal, prayerful communication between God and God's people. I've suggested that worship is a drama in three acts—preparing, hearing, and responding. Most, if not all, of acts one and three of worship are forms of prayer. Beyond that, if prayer is two-way communication between God and human, then act two may be understood as God praying through both the biblical word and preached word.

Consider how many elements in any authentic worship service are prayerful. In San Rafael's worship, there are three proscribed times of silence. Whether people are listening to the silence, opening themselves to God in the silence, or phrasing thoughts to God in the silence, we and God are praying together. Much of our worship is music, and much music is prayer in the form of melody. When we sing the lyrics, "Joyful, joyful, we adore you" or "Amazing grace, how sweet the sound, that saved a wretch like me," or "God of grace and God of glory, on your people pour your power," or "Precious Lord, take my hand," we are praying. We have silent and corporate prayers of praise, gratitude, confession, and dedication. In genuine worship, worshipers respond to hearing the Word of God by praying for God's world through prayers of lament, intercession, and dedication. Even our financial offerings are symbolic offerings of our prayerful gift of ourselves. Every aspect of worship is likely to elicit a prayerful response from some or all. Praying and worshiping are so close to being synonymous that it's hard to separate the two.

Prayer is particularly vital to the health and faithfulness of smaller congregations. It's easy for smaller churches to feel that they are irrelevant in the grand scale of things, as if God probably doesn't have an interest in listening to little old them, or as if their prayers are too meager to matter. Without the reassurance of prayer, a smaller church can easily fall into the trap of futility.

Larger churches have the financial and numerical clout to be movers and shakers, but efficacious prayer doesn't depend on dollars and numbers. Where two or three are gathered, Christ is among them. God is particularly anxious to find the lost sheep. Jesus noticed little Zaccheaus camouflaged in the sycamore tree and felt the anonymous touch of the hemorrhaging woman. Prayer is the transfusion that can save the life of the whole body. Prayer is the brook that connects those who pray to the sea that is God. Prayer makes even the smallest church a player in the divine drama. A small church that's fervent in its prayer can change the world as well as itself. Small churches are the right size for dynamic and effective prayer.

Larger churches pray differently than smaller churches. In larger churches, most of the praying is done by the professional and semi-professional pray-ers, while the audience listens in and maybe whispers a few footnotes. In larger churches, the prayers are more likely to be either lengthy compositions in the printed liturgy or carefully crafted extemporaneous prayers. Prayers in larger churches are inevitably more generic and less personalized. Often, larger churches will not do much of their praying in their formal worship but in smaller face-to-face groups, probably recognizing that praying is more organic when those who pray are in relationship.

Prayer in smaller churches is likely to be more the yearnings of the heart than constructions of the mind. It is likely to be less general and more situational and specific. It is likely to be less ritualized and more in the moment. In smaller churches, prayer is not only an effort to communicate with God, but with one another. In *The Cloister Walk*, Kathleen Norris writes about the powerful importance of prayer in the lives of the worshipers in the churches she knows in Hope and Spencer, South Dakota:

> people are asked to speak of any particular joys they wish to share with the congregation, or concerns they want us to address in our communal prayer on that Sunday, and also to pray over during the coming week. It's an invaluable part of our worship, a chance to discover things you didn't know: that the young woman sitting in the pew in front of you is desperately worried about her gravely ill brother in Oregon, that the widower in his eighties sitting across the aisle is overjoyed at the birth of his first great-grandchild.
>
> All of this pleases the gossips; I've been told that on Sunday afternoons the phone lines in town are hot with news that's been picked up at church. For the most part, it's a good kind of gossip, its main effect being to widen the prayer circle. It's useful news as well; I'm one of many who make notes on my church bulletin; so-and-so's in the hospital; send a card, plan a visit. Our worship sometimes goes into a kind of suspended animation, as people speak in great detail about the medical condition of their friends or relatives. We wince; we squirm; we sigh; and it's good for us. Moments like this are when the congregation is reminded of something that all pastors know; that listening is often the major part of ministry, that people in crisis need to tell their story, from beginning to end, and the best thing—often the only thing—that you can do is to sit there and take it in.
>
> And we do that pretty well. I sometimes feel that these moments are the heart of our worship.[26]

In smaller churches, whether the spoken prayers are offered by one person or in unison, the prayers are more the prayers of the whole church rather than individuals within the church. Dietrich Bonhoeffer counsels the Christian community to pray as a fellowship so that the whole body of Christ is praying, and each individual's prayer is an integral piece of the whole mosaic. There is great hope and power when we believe and experience that we aren't praying alone, but as a whole family.

So how do we nurture our churches into being communities of praying people rather than audiences of listeners? Guide people in understanding that worship is praying and that praying together is worship. Help them understand that authentic prayer is not something we initiate, but is our heart-felt response to what God has initiated. Make the place of worship a hospitable house of prayer where people can drop in any time to pray and find sanctuary. During the week, the front door might be unlocked and a visible sign might invite people in to pray. Make the content of worship real and current, not archaic or sweet-bye-and-bye. Know what's on your people's minds and hearts and help them know that whatever it is, it is appropriate content for prayer. Sing the hymns that put your people's feelings and prayers in verse and melody. Develop the spirit of sanctuary in your sanctuary so that people are free to speak their minds and bare their souls. Invite the concerns of the world into the sanctuary so that these concerns can be acknowledged and addressed. Don't have worship so finely tuned and orchestrated that opportunities for the human spirit and the divine Spirit to connect are squelched. Don't let worship be dominated by the professional preacher and prayer giver. Teach the people—adults and children—to pray in real words as expressions of honest feelings. Let there be joys and concerns. Pray for them, believing God hears and responds, heals and reconciles. Mobilize the community in assisting God in that responding. Don't stop praying when the worship ends.

There are concrete ways to help a smaller church become more of a praying church. If you are the pastor, announce that you will pray for a different church family every day of the week . . . and then do so. (And let the family of the day know that that is the day they're being prayed for.) Ask the congregation to pray for a different person or family in the church every week until you've gone through the whole list of church people. Then start over. Invite and encourage others besides the professionals to pray in worship. Use bidding prayers in which the leader names a subject or issue and bids the people to pray for each. Encourage more use of silence and silent prayer in worship. Have a time of joys and concerns if you don't already have one. Update the church on what has happened in the lives of those for whom they've prayed. Invite, encourage, and train people to write prayers of thanksgiving and confession, calls to worship, responses for your liturgy. Have a Bible study on prayer passages in the Bible. Develop a prayer chain of people willing to take intercession seriously, train them, pray with them, and develop a simple notification system.

If our smaller churches are to know, believe, and experience that they are not superfluous in God's wider community, they must become a prayer-full people. Only then will they feel connected, in touch, able, and needed. Only then will they know that they are making a difference and must keep on keeping on. Remind them that "the way we pray the liturgy expresses our faith and hope in God's new creation, and the love by which we both grow and are recreated into God's people."[27]

Questions:

1. When, how, and for what does your church pray? Does anyone besides the pastor pray out loud?
2. How do you and how do they understand prayer?

Suggestion:

Announce, plan, and promote a prayer meeting and see who comes and what happens. If no one comes, announce, plan, and promote a school of prayer and see who comes and what happens.

PRACTICE #12: Customize the Sacraments and Make Them Up-Close and Personal

The water of baptism, the bread and wine of communion, have in the "respectable" churches become symbolic substitutes for the true presence of Christ in the sacramental performance. Originally, we should suppose, the water, bread, and wine belonged to rituals in which persons were ecstatically possessed by a power they identified as "The risen Christ.". . . Sometimes the presence of God in worship is palpable. Every act that brings this about is, in general terms, "sacramental," even if it is not one of the specific sacraments recognized by tradition.[28]

Growing up Baptist, we had two ordinances—baptism and communion. The church stressed the remembering of Jesus' baptism and his Lord's supper instructions that we should do this in memory of him, and so we did. The churches I grew up in (which were larger) were better at baptizing (immersion) than they were at communion (little Wonder Bread cubes and thimbles of grape juice).

United Church of Christ churches observe the same two customs but call them sacraments. We believe that through the water of baptism and ingestion of bread and wine or grape juice, God is present and acting in some real, powerful, and mysterious way to cleanse, heal, initiate, transform, and build the local and global community of God. The purpose here is not to debate sacramental theology. Rather, I'm suggesting that our churches have watered down (pun intended) baptism from its pivotal place in early church history. And, in many of our churches' communion practices, we've filtered out the yeast in the wine and bread, resulting in a flat and pallid reenactment of what is designed to be an incarnational and transformative encounter between God and human.

Early in church history, both baptism and the Lord's Supper were powerful practices in which the spirit of God was palpably present, when participants were changed, and when the local church was empowered for its mission in an often hostile world. Now, in many churches, baptism is a warm, domesticated photo-op for families, many of whom we never see again. Clergy who do the sprinkling often use as little water as possible in order not to rouse a sleeping baby or dampen the carpet. The liturgy is often a rote and generic reading from the denominational worship book. Often the Lord's Supper feels like a post-script which is infrequently tacked on to the end of the service and kept short enough so the worshipers can get home to their real dinner. How sad! Because we are the right size to be personal, we are the right size to do better and to be more faithful in our sacramental life. We are the right size to customize our sacramental acts and to perform them in ways that enable our people to get up close and personal with their God and one another and to catch the vision of what God has in store for all of us.

There's much that's wrong in how we practice our sacramental life. We are *too individualistic*. Some people ask for a private baptism, and some pastors and churches acquiesce. Baptism is often interpreted as an individual transaction between God, the baptized, the family, and the pastor rather than as an initiation into the local and global Body of Christ and Community of God. Too often, communion emphasizes the individual communing with God rather than a family meal around a table open to and large enough for all of God's children which is a rehearsal for the great cosmic banquet for the whole Community of God from all times and places. The elements are individualized and sanitized into thimbles and pre-cut bits of something resembling bread. One entrepreneur has created airtight, two pocket packets with a cracker-like pellet and two grams of grape juice, resulting in a sterile and disposable Lord's Supper. There's little comprehension among those who administer and those who participate in the sacraments that the intent of the sacrament is not personal edification, but rather communal and global transformation.

What we do in our sacramental lives is *too passive*. The spectators watch the clergy apply water to someone (often barely known) and smile approvingly while they wait for the service to get back to the normal routine. When it's time for communion, the clergy, who are up front, announces, breaks, pours, prays, says mystical things, and then sends carefully oriented and serious assistants out among the faithful (sometimes restricted to members of their own branch of Christendom) to quietly deliver a little bread and juice that's not enough to wet anyone's whistle or whet anyone's appetite. Some churches invite the congregants to come to the front to receive their taste. Some allow the laity to play a more substantive role. And some make the sacramental action a more active, dramatic, and meal-like endeavor.

What we do in our sacramental lives is *too parochial.* Too often pastors and congregations believe they've been appointed as the gatekeepers and monitors of God's amazing graces. Many won't baptize any but their own or welcome into membership any who've not been *properly* baptized. In some churches the invitation to the table is more an announcement of who's not welcome to commune at the Lord's table. Churches often bar children from the table because it's believed they don't know enough or haven't progressed to the level of church indoctrination that warrants the perk of communion.

I believe that God, in ways far beyond my comprehension, is actively present and working when we participate in sacramental actions. In fact, the belief that God is present and active is part of the definition of *sacrament.* That being the case, I won't be the one who keeps anyone away from a possible encounter with the Holy One when we administer the sign and substance of water, wine, and bread. I will baptize anyone or the child of anyone who requests baptism, providing they come into our corporate worship and understand that baptism is the doorway into the local and global church and something God does as a sign and seal of divine love. Even when I question the motives of the parents, I'm reluctant to withhold the graces of baptism from a child. The only time I have administered a private baptism is when our board of ministry and I took baptism to the bedside of a dying four-year-old.

Throughout my ministry, our churches have opened the Lord's table to anyone who wishes to be there. Our children are particularly welcome. John Westerhoff suggests that communion is a mystery no one fully understands, and that since children understand mystery far more than we adults, they should be especially included.[29] Perhaps they can help us better appreciate the mystery that's unfolding around the table. The Lord's table is the family dinner table of the people of God. That being the case, there's a dual reason the table must be open to all. First, Jesus, who is the Lord, ate and drank with anyone and everyone who wanted to eat and drink with him. His table was never closed. Second, we are taught from Genesis 18 to Hebrews 13 to always extend hospitality to the stranger, if for no other reason than when we welcome the stranger we may, in fact, be welcoming the Holy One.

Finally, the way we live out our sacramental life is *too routine and lacks imagination.* Denominational books of worship provide little variety in orders for baptism and celebrations of communion. Too often our baptism liturgy is the boilerplate version we use for everyone, personalized only by the insertion of the name of the baptized. Too often our communion liturgy is the same boilerplate version throughout the church year. Some may feel the repetitive or rote nature of the liturgy allows them to delve more deeply into its nuances and mystery. This may be true for some, but I believe that for many others, the repetition sooner or later breeds immunity from the transforming power of the sacrament.

So what can we do in our smaller sacramental settings to make our liturgies more communal and less individualistic, more dynamic and less passive, more personal and less generic, more imaginative and less routine? Plenty. A first step is to recognize that our sacraments were most powerful and revelatory when they were practiced by the smaller, first and second century churches, and to seek to replicate what made them so. The early church baptized those who had completed a rigorous time of preparation. Its baptisms were special occasions, often held on the Saturday night before Easter morning. Over time, baptisms were moved from lakes and rivers, to pools, to something resembling a bird-bath, to smaller and smaller bowls (often hidden in a closet or covered until needed). Was it coincidental that as the water source was diminished, the power of the practice also was likewise diminished and trivialized?

In the same way, we've diminished and trivialized the sacrament of communion. The earliest churches gathered weekly in someone's home for fellowship, to pray, to receive the teaching of the apostles and elders, and to share an agape meal together. The earliest churches ate of one yeasty loaf; most Christians today get a tasteless wafer or a pallid tablet. The earliest churches shared one large chalice or goblet around the common table. Most Christians today are individually served a mere taste of the fruit of the vine. A church would do well to have its liturgical leaders, lay and clergy, do a careful study of 1 Corinthians 10 and 11 to see what the sacrament of communion was meant to be and how easily it can be diluted by increased numbers and the press of other matters.

William Willimon, in *Sunday Dinner*, a book on the Lord's Supper and the Christian life, points to the relevance of size: "Larger churches sometimes claim that Communion is difficult for them because they have so many people to serve or it takes too long." He goes on to proclaim: "If a church is too big to serve people, too big for people to fellowship with one another and with Christ on a regular basis, a church is too big to be a church!"[30] If your church has fewer than one hundred worshipers, it has the advantage of being the right size to have a sacramental life that is full of life and is life giving.

Baptism starts with the water. Frankly, as a former Baptist, I miss immersion and a baptistery that's big enough to be drowned in the old life and bathed into new life. But that's not part of my adopted United Church of Christ tradition, so I have to be imaginative. Our church just completed a dramatic rebuilding of our sanctuary which allows us to think not just aesthetically but theologically about our sacred space for worship. Historically, the baptismal pool or font was at the door of the church to remind worshipers that it is through the waters of baptism that we enter the church. We considered that option, but chose to place our baptismal fountain in front of the sanctuary (which will almost be in the center of the people) so that we can be reminded not just when we enter and leave, but throughout worship that it is through the waters of baptism that we come into the Christian life and community and that, as baptized persons, we are endlessly called to a life of discipleship. We have given the baptismal font or fountain the same prominence as the communion table and the pulpit, to remind us that Word and Sacrament are equally important, interrelated, and efficacious. After much discussion, we decided to have our font be a fountain with moving water to remind us that Christ is living water and offers fresh water from a bottomless well that quenches all thirst. We are able to hear the water moving and see the water since it's not in a tiny bowl, but in a vessel large enough that we could dip the baptized person's head or at least provide a good handful of water. Architecturally and liturgically we have moved baptism out of the closet and into the center of our liturgical life.

Now that the water is up front, visible, and living, how can we use it to make baptism personal? In seven years in San Rafael, I've only baptized about a dozen people, which means we can personalize each baptism and make it special and memorable. I meet with the one being baptized or the parents if it's a child being baptized. We talk about what it means to the individual or the family and how we in the Christian tradition understand baptism. We talk about the nature of the Christian community and what that community can mean to the baptized and her or his family. If we're baptizing a child, this conversation ought to happen with the child present so we can't possibly lose sight of our commitment to the nurture of that precious gift.

I won't baptize more than one person in a service (unless siblings are being baptized) so that the church can focus on that particular person and our unique relationship to him or her. A special customized baptism order of worship is created for each baptism. We print the baptismal certificate on the cover, but with the magic of a good copier and, perhaps, digital photography, the cover could be a photo of the one being baptized. The baptized or the family of the baptized can help write the liturgy. It can and should be customized to fit the person, family, and church that are partners in this sacramental act.

Although baptism is more appropriate after we hear the Word read and preached, we want our church's children present so baptism takes place at the time of the children's story. They are invited to the front. They could be enlisted to help fill the font with water. If the congregation is fewer than twenty or thirty, everyone could be invited to come and circle around. As a congregation, we serenade the one being baptized with words sung to the tune of "Morning Has Broken."

(First name), we name you: And with thanksgiving,
Offer our prayer and sing you this song.
We are the church, your spiritual family.
Sing we our praises to Christ the Lord.

(Second verse) Children we all are, of God the creator;
Risking and loving, daring to see
The heavenly kingdom growing among us.
Sing we our praises to Christ the Lord.

As in a wedding, the baptized or the family of the baptized makes vows or promises. Godparents make promises. The church makes promises. The church can provide a sponsor or godparent to insure that the church keeps the promises it makes to the baptized and family. When a child known to the church is being baptized, the congregation can be asked to bring cards and letters containing a prayer, blessing, or hope that is read aloud and then given to the family to be saved and shared with the baptized at a later time. The church can give a symbolic gift to the child to help this be a remembered day. The gift could be a baptism tree that will grow as the baptized grows and matures. In addition, the baptized or family of the baptized could participate in the rest of the service. There could be a party afterwards in her or his honor. Finally, at the end of the baptism liturgy, I cup a handful of water and cast it out over the congregation with the admonition to: "Remember your own baptism!" If we're serious about this thing called faith and discipleship, we must make baptism as memorable an event in the life of the baptized and the church as his or her biological birth was and death will be.

John Westerhoff once witnessed a baptism in a small Latin American church. The church had gathered and recalled God's gracious acts. Now they were ready to respond. The congregation began a mournful funeral hymn as a solemn procession moved to the front. A father carried a child's coffin he had made; a mother carried a bucket of water from the family well; a priest carried their sleeping infant. The father placed the coffin on the altar, the mother emptied the bucket into the coffin, the priest covered the baby's skin with embalming oil. The singing quieted to a whisper. The priest lowered the infant into the coffin and immersed the child's head. He exclaimed: "I kill you in the name of the Father and of the Son and of the Holy Spirit." "Amen!" shouted the parents and congregation. Quickly lifting the child into the air, the priest exclaimed, "And I resurrect you that you might love and serve the Lord." The congregation burst into a joyous Easter hymn. The priest then covered the child with the oils of birth and dressed the child in a homemade robe. As the singing quieted, the priest made the sign of the cross on the child's forehead and said: "I brand you with the sign of Christ so that you and the world will always know who you are and to whom you belong." The singing then continued as all the people came forward to share the kiss of peace with the newest member of their family.[31] If we don't dramatize and empower baptism in that way, then we must find our own equally powerful and indigenous ritual for baptizing people into the cost and joy of Christian discipleship.

What about the Lord's Supper? In each church I've served, communion had previously been more of an afterthought than a core practice. In each church, I worked with the leaders to change that. We started with educating the congregation about the sacraments. While liturgical scholars are unanimous in pronouncing that Christian worship is incomplete without communion, most Protestants don't commune weekly. Use whatever leverage you have to see that the church communes at least monthly or more often and then work to make sure it's worth doing more often. If it's done well enough, the people may clamor for more frequent communing. (Imagine that!)

Educate the community that what it's doing in remembrance of Jesus is the Passover family meal Jesus shared with those he most loved, as well as God's eschatological banquet for the whole family of God, so they know that this is their holy family meal. Figure out how to make it seem like a family meal. Make the sacrament the climax of the Sunday liturgy, not the footnote or postscript. Shorten the sermon. Get rid of the wafers and Wonder Bread and have a baker in the church bake real, tasty, textured bread. In Warwick, our bakers took turns baking our communion bread. Ask a Sunday school class or the confirmation class to bake the bread. Perhaps a member with a few grape vines will make the grape juice or wine. A tradition in our late Christmas eve communion service is a braided wreath of red and white of bread. The bread is almost reason enough to stay up late to be there.

When I came to San Rafael, I inherited a wonderful communion ritual. The rest of the service is shortened so the communion drama takes center stage. The table is always at the front and center of the chancel, not against the back wall. The table was designed as a family dinner table. It is often covered with a white or lace table cloth to remind us that this is God's great banquet. All God's people who wish are invited to come forward, passing the Peace of Christ as they form a circle around the table. Our children come back from church school to join their parents in the circle.

We sing a haunting chant two or three times: "Gathered here in the mystery of this hour, gathered here in one strong body, gathered here in the struggle and the power, Spirit draw near." Being mindful of the season of the church year and what is going on in our church life and the world, I talk about the meaning of the sacrament for us in this time and place. One delicious loaf of bread and two pottery chalices, a bread paten, and a carafe, which have been made for this congregation, are on the family dinner table. Words of institution and a prayer are offered. Then, in two pairs, we take bread and chalice around the circle, and our people are invited to tear off and dip a piece of bread in the chalice and then eat. Occasionally, people are invited to bring and name imaginary others to the table—one who has died, one who is missing from the circle, others for whom we are concerned. Recently, one of our men brought the sixth billionth person who was to have been born that week. Our service ends with prayer and a unison singing of "Shalom" as we hold hands, lifting them at the end. Our new chancel was designed to accommodate this form of sharing the Lord's Supper.

I tailor communion to the church year: making it more penitential and focused on the Last Supper during Lent; very celebrative after Easter and focused on the Emmaus story; focused on the universal church family and the Spirit among us during the season of Pentecost. On Maundy Thursday, the congregation has participated in an authentic Jewish seder ending with a eucharistic drinking from the Elijah cup and eating Matzoh bread; a catacomb service in a church or parishioner's basement to reenact an early church worship, when songs were sung and stories of Jesus were shared from memory, and we shared the Lord's Supper as we remembered Jesus doing it; an agape meal around white table clothed tables; a foot washing service and communion; and a dramatic reenactment of the Last Supper.

There is always a special communion service on World Communion Sunday (the first Sunday in October). We remember and celebrate that, in theory, all Christian churches are also gathering around the Lord's Table around the world. People are invited to come in dress from other cultures. Liturgical readings and hymns from different languages and cultures are used. Breads from different cultures are used.

A communion service could be shared as a Sunday brunch in the church dining room around tables or the banquet room of a neighborhood restaurant. I can imagine reenacting meals from the gospels, such as a loaves and fishes service by a lake, or publicans and sinners dinner party with the one dramatizing Jesus reaching out to the outcasts while asking hard questions of the pious.

Two commercial films beautifully illustrate the power of food and drink to transform persons and build community. I've used clips from each to heighten the understanding of what is happening when the Christian community comes around its family table. One film is *Babette's Feast*, set in Norway in the late 1800s. Two elderly ladies in an austere, dying sect, which has renounced the pleasures of this world, have taken in a mysterious French woman named Babette to be their maid and cook. She cooks and cleans for them for twelve years. She discovers that a friend has been buying a lottery ticket for her yearly and that she has won a ten-thousand franc prize. Babette asks permission to use this money to prepare a real French banquet for the little community to celebrate the one-hundredth anniversary of the birth of the community's founder. With great trepidation about luxury and waste, the sisters consent, and Babette spends weeks preparing for the feast. The pious community agrees to attend the banquet, but they also agree among themselves to keep it a somber and sober occasion.

The Sunday evening arrives and the community of twelve gather. With frozen faces, they come around the table and the banquet commences. Course after exquisite course is served. The wonderful food and fine wine begin to thaw the frosty atmosphere. Despite their best efforts, the guests begin to enjoy themselves. There is talk of grace. Through the meal, epiphany and revelation happen, the eyes of the sect are opened to core aspects of the gospel they had missed. Thanks to the banquet, there is reason to hope that the dying community might come alive. Isak Dinesen wrote of what happened in *Babette's Feast*, which is what happens whenever true sacrament is experienced: "The moment of epiphany happens when time and eternity, human art and divine creativity together meet to illumine each other so that the human participants might grasp the true oneness in God of all creation."[32]

Another film uses a small town, small church communion service to portray a vision and possibility that the Lord's Table can be the place where all are welcome, where divisions are healed, where genuine community is born. *Places in the Heart*, starring Sally Field, takes place in Texas in the 1930s. The film begins when the sheriff, the husband of the Sally Field character, is shot and killed by a drunk black youth. The film is full of prejudice, violence, and oppression—against blacks, women, the disabled. The plot centers in Sally Field's valiant effort to save the family farm. She takes in a homeless black field hand and a blind young man. The bank tries to foreclose on the farm and the elevator operator tries to cheat her as she seeks to grow a cotton crop against great odds.

Something mysteriously incredible happens in the last scene. The scene is a sparsely attended worship service. 1 Corinthians 13 is read. The participants in a broken marriage lean toward one another and take hands. The communion elements are passed. People who were missing are suddenly present. The four Klansmen are there with the black field hand they had beaten and they exchange elements. The uncaring banker and the unscrupulous grain elevator operator are present and participating. Sally's dead husband is present and sitting beside the young man who had shot him and they pass the Peace of Christ to one another.

I showed this scene in worship as the Invitation to the Lord's Table and then said to our congregation: "You are invited this morning to a very special table. You can bring whomever you wish with you. Bring someone you've lost through anger, hurt, moving away, death. Bring someone you miss. There are others you could bring. Bring a peasant from El Salvador or an Arab you've been taught to hate. Bring those from a church who won't commune with us. Bring whomever you like. Bring those persons and find healing and wholeness at the table of the Lord. And let our table, God's Table, always be open to any and all."

As the quote at the beginning of this section suggested, some liturgical acts are so powerful or the need for powerful acts so necessary, that we are called upon to create sacramental or sacramental-like liturgies. Well-done weddings and end-of-life rituals feel sacramental. Our confirmation ritual, including a congregational laying on of hands, certainly has sacramental power. We should be ready with a sacrament-like ritual whenever important events occur or needs become apparent in the lives of our people, community, and world. Sacramental acts are distinctive, needed gifts the Church has to give the world. Smaller worshiping communities can offer them with particular poignancy.

Questions:

1. What sacramental experiences have been most memorable for you?
2. What ideas do you have for making your church's sacramental observances more powerful and spirit-filled?

Suggestion:

Invite people to come together to swap stories of humorous, wonderful, or intriguing sacramental experiences and invite conversation about ways of breathing new life and meaning into your traditional observances of the sacraments. Then share the bread and cup.

PRACTICE #13: The Worship Space Shapes the Worship and the People

Genesis 28:10–19 [Story of Jacob wrestling with God]—"Surely the Lord is in this place—and I did not know it! . . . How awesome is this place! This is none other than the house of God." . . . He called that place Bethel.

. . . the place becomes an inexhaustible source of power and sacredness and enables man, simply by entering it, to have a share in the power, to hold communion with the sacredness[33]

[A widow talking to her pastor] "For thirty-eight years I shared that pew with my husband . . . I feel God is closer to me there than anywhere else. There is no place like that pew on earth."[34]

The church building is a prime aid, or a prime hindrance, to the building up of the Body of Christ. . . . And the building will always win.[35]

The places where small churches worship are as varied as the Christian Church itself, ranging from living rooms to cavernous sanctuaries that once housed large congregations. In small churches the room for worship is often the only room in the building, and, if not the only one, it's usually the principal room.

For many the worship room offers a real sense of sanctuary or safe and holy place in the midst of a threatening secular world. Whether it is good theology or not, many people feel God is somehow more present or approachable there than in the world at large. Inside the holy place are holy things. Some are obvious like the cross, the Bible, the altar. Other holy things not so obvious might be a picture, vase, piano, or organ. . . . The holy place is full of clues for the curious and land mines for the unsuspecting.

For many, it's the place where they've gone almost every Sunday of their lives, where they were married, where a son was baptized and a daughter confirmed, from where a parent or spouse was buried. It's a place of refuge, comfort, decision, security, and hope. It's where some of their best friends are. It's a place some have helped build, furnish, and maintain, while others have paid dearly to keep it open. For many, it is the most orderly, attractive, peaceful, and hospitable place in an otherwise chaotic, drab, stressful, and hostile world. Although it may appear modest to the visitor, the place is very important to those who worship there, and even to many who don't.[36]

These quotations illustrate how very important place is to the people and worship of smaller congregations. In fact, the place of worship is often more important in smaller congregations than in larger ones. It generally takes up a larger percentage of the total square footage of the facility and houses more people each week than any other part of the building. It's likely that a larger percentage of the people have worshiped there for a longer time than in larger churches (where people tend to come and go more frequently). Therefore, they are more at home and rooted in that space. What happens in that room is the primary church activity for the people who reside there. Because the God they worship is more immanent than transcendent, they are more likely to experience their place as holy in the way Jacob experienced Bethel and Eliade philosophized about.

Church buildings and holy places are very much in my mind. I recently participated in a remarkable tour of historical and religious sites in Turkey, a country with over seven thousand years of archeological history. Most of that history is centered in places so holy that different religions have claimed and occupied the same spaces. In Istanbul, the magnificent St. Sophia was an Orthodox cathedral before it became an Islamic mosque, and the Christian frescoes are still present. We worshiped in Antioch of Pisidia on the excavated floor of the synagogue where the Apostle Paul preached the first recorded Christian sermon in the western world, and where a Christian church was built upon the ruins of the synagogue. In the magnificent city of Ephesus, within a stone's throw of one another, you can find the Greek Temple of Artemis, the Roman Temple of Hadrian, the Christian Church of the Virgin Mary (site of the Third Ecumenical Council), and close by is the Isabey Mosque and the Church of St. John. Some of this building-of-holy-place-upon-holy-place is due to the scavenging of building materials and one religion supplanting another. But it was clear that, through the centuries, certain places were believed to have an inherent aura of sacredness while others remained barren of sacred meaning.

The other reason sacred places are much on my mind comes from spending six years planning and renovating the San Rafael church and especially the worship space. The sanctuary, built in 1960, was very utilitarian, all brown, long and narrow, poorly lit and poorly amplified, fronted by a chancel clogged with screwed down, nondescript furnishings. Little was distinctive about it except for the lattice cross, which was gloriously decorated with fresh flowers on Easter and looked rather peculiar the rest of the year. The space encouraged a passive, leader-spectator style of worship.

The renovation took six years because we needed to renovate other spaces first, because our people have a pay-as-you-go approach, and because we listened long and hard to everyone as we worked and studied to determine what we wanted to accomplish and how we could best achieve those objectives. It was necessary for us to understand what worship is and how our worship space could best facilitate our understanding. We thought about the story (cited earlier) of the two men studying the magnificent cathedral of Amiens, France and one saying, "In those days people had convictions. We moderns have opinions. It takes more than opinions to build a Gothic cathedral." So we moved beyond our opinions to our convictions. We worked to create a sanctuary that communicates and facilitates both who we are and what we believe. It was very exciting watching the new sanctuary evolve.

Early in our sanctuary renovation process, we created a design committee composed of people who agreed to study both the theology and practicality of sacred space. After reading several provocative articles and using them to enlighten our views of worship, as well as our perception of our needs, we settled on twelve principles that would shape the reconstruction of our sanctuary. These principles could be used by any congregation thinking seriously about their worship space.

1. There should be equality and a dynamic relationship between the pulpit where the Word of God is heard, the table where the Body of Christ enjoys the sacrament of the Lord's Supper, and the font where the Spirit of God receives us into the community of God through the sacrament of baptism.
2. The sanctuary should communicate a distinctive difference between sacred and secular space.
3. The space should facilitate a communal, not individualized, worship experience.
4. It should encourage an active, not passive, response from the people of God.
5. The sanctuary, through arrangement and symbolism, should communicate what we believe and are called to be and do.
6. The nature of the space should reflect the nature of this congregation and be indigenous to it.
7. The arrangement should be highly flexible, suitable for different uses by different groups, but be primarily for Christian worship.
8. The musicians and instruments should lead our music without being the center of attention.
9. The whole space should be accessible to all of God's people.
10. The space should be planned with visitors and the future church in mind, not just the present membership.
11. Our sanctuary should be aesthetically and sensitively beautiful.
12. Our focus should be on a quality worship experience more than worship for a quantity of people.

These principles guided the planning of the sanctuary and have been realized in the finished product. The new sanctuary is dramatically transforming our worship and our people, making both our ministry and mission more faithful and effective.

These twelve principles could be useful to any church that wants its worship space to better serve both the intentions of Christian worship and the needs of its people. They can guide an evaluation of current worship space. They might help a congregation as it thinks about sprucing up its worship space or rearranging its furnishings. And they would be helpful to a congregation planning to rearrange, remodel, rebuild, or build a new sanctuary. I've been in hundreds of sanctuaries. Many are attractive, some are beautiful, but few really inspire and facilitate the transformation of mind and spirit for the ministry and mission to which God is calling the congregation.

A church's worship space deserves careful consideration because it has enormous influence on what does and does not happen there. More than we know, we are shaped, helped, or hindered by the spaces we occupy. When a congregation of twenty or fifty worshipers rattle around in a sanctuary built and furnished for two hundred or five hundred, it will be exceedingly difficult for them to feel like a cohesive and powerful community. When a congregation worships in a space that's drab and dreary, it will be difficult for them to have more than a drab and dreary faith. When a congregation tries to worship in a space that was planned for an earlier congregation and in which everything is immovable and untouchable, it's very difficult for the present church to feel at home and energized. If people cannot see and hear, their minds and hearts will easily wander to other places. If all they see is the back of other people's heads, it's unlikely they will actively worship as an interactive community. J. A. T. Robinson was right: "The church building is a prime aid, or a prime hindrance, to the building up of the Body of Christ. . . . And the building will always win."[37]

Virtually any worship space can be made a more faithful and effective place for doing the liturgical work of the people. Follow these progressive steps:

- Define who you uniquely are as a people of faith.
- Define what you as a whole church believe about worship and faith.
- List what you want to have happen when you gather for worship.
- Evaluate how your current worship space accommodates what you've just said about your selves, faith, and worship.
- Brainstorm and specify what you might do and would like to do to accommodate your space to what you believe should happen in it. (List every idea without regard to practicality, cost, or whether there is consensus.)
- Now you need to test your ideas, prioritize, consider the practical questions (like cost), determine the will of your people, strategize how to proceed, and take the first steps.

From most basic to most adventurous, here is a list of actions that can make a real difference in how effectively worship happens in your worship space.

- Have an all church work party to clean your worship space: throw away accumulated clutter, sweep away the cobwebs, wash the windows, dust every surface, polish the furniture, replace the light bulbs with a little more wattage.
- Repaint the sanctuary, refinish the furniture, replace the carpet.
- Improve the sound system (being able to hear in church is a right, not a privilege).
- Do something to improve the seating and communal nature of worship: Rope off or remove back pews you don't use; unscrew the

pews and move them into a herringbone arrangement or semi-circle so people can see and communicate with one another; consider replacing pews with chairs (though we chose to keep our pews because they are better for cuddling children, squeezing in one more, being communal).

- Lower the chancel platform, move the communion table to the front of the chancel, remove any structural barriers between worship leaders and worshipers so that the audience become actors in the divine drama and worship leaders (clergy, choir, lay leaders) are part of and interactive with the rest of the community.

- If this does not accomplish your ends or your people are truly adventurous, remodel, renovate, rebuild, or build from scratch.

If one of these last options is the best one for you, get your most thoughtful and creative people to participate in a study of sacred space, study provocative documents about sacred space, visit other churches of a similar size to see what you like and don't like, then hire a really good architect (one who understands sacred and communal space) and trust him or her. Our architect led our church in two workshops to determine what we wanted and to test possible ideas. Don't assume you can't afford to renovate or build until you test this assumption by canvassing your church and conducting a serious and challenging fund raising campaign. We thought our original goal of $100,000 was a fantasy. In fact, the renovation of our whole facility cost $500,000, and we borrowed less than $100,000. We are in almost 100 percent agreement that it was worth every penny. You can save a considerable amount of money by using the time and talents of your people and they will feel more invested. We received at least $100,000 worth of donated labor from our congregation. As much as possible, do your very best to see that your worship space fits your worship rather than having your worship fit your worship space. Once you're finished, advertise it, celebrate it, and use it for the glorification of God and the strengthening of the whole people of God.

Long ago a traveler from Italy came to Chartres, France, to see the great new church being built there. Arriving at the end of the work day, the traveler entered the church as the workers were putting things away. He asked one dust covered worker what he did there. He said he was a stone mason who spent each day carving stone. He asked another who said he was a glassblower who spent his days making, cutting, and fitting pieces of glass. Another said he was a blacksmith who pounded iron all day. Wandering deep into the gloom of the unfinished church, the traveler encountered an older woman, sweeping up stone chips, wood shavings, and glass shards. "What are you doing?" he asked. The woman paused, leaned on her broom, looked up at the soaring arches and replied, "Me? I'm building a cathedral for the Glory of Almighty God." No matter how small or modest your church, you can do much to make it a cathedral for the glory of God and the wonderful worship of the people of God. That intent makes all the difference in the world!

Questions:

1. How does your present worship space hinder or help the worship of your people?
2. How does it fall short of or fulfill the twelve principles for worship space listed in this chapter?

Suggestions:

1. Gather a group of your people and ask them to share their experiences of other sacred spaces in other places. Where have they most felt the presence of God and been affected by it? Then discuss the virtues and problems of your sacred space.
2. Initiate at least one significant improvement of your worship space and test openness to additional improvements.

PRACTICE #14: Worship So People Leave Feeling Healed, Affirmed, Equipped, and Called

Our culture is a working, hurrying, and worrying culture with many opportunities except the opportunity to celebrate life.[38]

Worship ushers us into the presence of the living God and demands the attention, receptivity, and response of our whole being. It asks us to disengage from the nose-length focus of daily life and see below the surface to life's source. We can then reengage the realities of the world from a deeper and clearer perspective.[39]

Life is hard. Whether there are two or three or one hundred present, the room is bursting with need. Some are physically ill. Others are experiencing mental or spiritual anguish. Some are angry—at family, friends, you, life, God, self. Some are in financial crisis. And others are in family crisis. Some are feeling all alone while others are desperate for some solitude. Some are working too hard and others hardly working. Others are almost paralyzed with fear. Some are feeling worthless while others are overwhelmed. Some are foundering in the face of an impending future. There may be a few who're on top of the world, whole and healthy. The worship leader who is fully cognizant of the depth of need present waiting to be addressed will exhibit great courage simply by not fleeing. The wise and sensitive pastor who's in tune with the congregation will plan and facilitate a worship experience that heals, affirms, equips, and calls the needy to new life and faithful discipleship. While we can't do that every time for every person, if we don't try we are shortchanging our calling and our people.

The primary purpose in gathering people for holy worship is not to per-petuate an institution, to merely provide one more worship service, or to flaunt a flair for impressing people. The principle purpose is to be the host who brings God and God's guests together for a celebration of life in all its fullness, so that God is worthily honored and God's guests are renewed and equipped to live again. Whether we are friend, spouse, or parent, we experience how difficult it is to address the essential need of just one other person. How then can we do that when we're faced by up to a hundred very different and very needy per-sons? We do it the same way we would eat an elephant—very carefully, and one bite at a time. The genius of Christian worship and the wonder of God's grace is that in the space of an hour or so, a room full of needy people can have their essential need met. How, you ask?

Knowing we have people present who are hungry for genuine community, we create opportunity for them to transcend their individualness and connect with one another. We do that by inviting people to stand up, move around, and greet one another. We do that by having multiple opportunities for corporate sharing and singing so they experience their voices blending with other voices to form one strong and beautiful voice. We do that through praising the God who is creating us for community and offering confessions that shed the pre-tenses that separate us. We do that by connecting with a spiritual tradition through hearing and reflecting upon God's Word and the preached word, both of which help us discover that neither in our folly nor our faithfulness are we alone. We do that by exchanging good and bad news of one another and the world and holding one another and the world in prayer. We do that by giving gifts that will sustain and expand our shared life. We do that through sacraments that welcome one another into God's baptized family and call us all to our place around God's abundant table.

We have people hungry for solitude, so we honor the need for silence and quiet reflection. Recognizing there are various forms of sickness, fear, and alien-ation among us, we offer carefully articulated prayers that trust that God does care, answer, heal, reconcile, encourage, and equip in God's own way. Knowing we are facing many folks who feel inadequate to live up to what's expected of them, we offer a liturgy of hope, words of affirmation, sacraments of promise. Aware that life is difficult for most of our people, and that they question the adequacy of their personal resources, we use biblical resources with which they can identify and utilize religious practices that have long addressed the deepest needs of seeking people. Since it's God's job to judge and our job simply to love with wise compassion, the worship leader who uses the worship hour as a time to scold or shame is guilty of pastoral abuse. Finally, whether or not we're from an evangelical tradition that employs an altar call, we are responsible for creating a liturgy that confronts people with God's expectation, that calls them to leave different than they arrived, and that gives them the opportunity to make new promises of faithfulness.

If we don't build into worship the expectation that people will leave as healed, affirmed, equipped, and called people, they won't, and we will have squandered our call to be their pastor and priest.

Question:

Examine last Sunday's order of worship, sermon, and the spontaneous happenings of the service to determine whether and how the needy people who were present may have been helped to feel healed, affirmed, equipped, and called.

Suggestion:

Take time in a gathering of your people to invite them to share memories of worship services which deeply touched their need and helped them to live again. Ask what could be done to allow this to happen more often and for more people.

PRACTICE #15: Be a Home of Hospitality Where Every Visitor Is a Guest Who Wants to Return

> Sometimes you want to go where everybody knows your
> name and is always glad you came.
> —Theme song from TV program *Cheers*

In our world full of strangers, estranged from their own past, culture and country, from their neighbors, friends and family, from their deepest self and their God, we witness a painful search for a hospitable place where life can be lived without fear and where community can be found . . . it is . . . obligatory for Christians to offer an open and hospitable space where strangers can cast off their strangeness and become our fellow human beings . . . that is our vocation: to convert the hostis into a hospes, the enemy into a guest and to create the free and fearless space where brotherhood and sisterhood can be formed and fully experienced.[40]

It's been estimated that every week fifty-three thousand people drop out of church involvement. Why? I'm sure there are many reasons, but I imagine the principle reason people leave churches is because they don't feel at home, they don't find churches to be hospitable places where they want to be. Many churches are small because too many have found them to be inhospitable. This is unfortunate since they are the right size to be places where everybody knows [or learns] your name and is glad you came. The principle time when people experience whether or not a church is hospitable or hostile is before, during, and after the worship event.

I wrote an article for *The Five Stones* (a fine quarterly by and for folks in smaller churches) titled "The Moth Principle of Church Attraction." I suggested that people are like moths who naturally flock to light and warmth and that churches which project light and exude warmth will have people gravitating to them out of darkness and coldness. So how can our smaller churches become places and people who project light and exude warmth?

First, it's a matter of belief. Do the people believe genuine hospitality is a mandate or merely an option? The Old Testament Law in Leviticus 19:33–34 requires hospitality: "The alien who resides with you shall be to you as the citizen among you; you shall love the alien as yourself, for you were aliens in the land of Egypt." We are to welcome others in grateful response to our having been once welcomed ourselves. Jesus requires of us that we welcome others in the same spirit and manner we would welcome him if he came among us (Mt. 25:31–46). This teaching of Jesus is a primary principle in the monastic Rule of St. Benedict: "All guests to the monastery should be welcomed as Christ, because He will say, 'I was a stranger, and you took me in.'" Paul instructed the Roman churches and all churches: "Extend hospitality to strangers" (Rom. 12:13). Hebrews 13:2 reminds the churches of the benefit of being hospitable: "Do not neglect to show hospitality to strangers, for by so doing that some have entertained angels without knowing it."

Several years ago, I came to California from New England to visit my mother who was hospitalized. I decided to worship at both her Baptist church and the UCC church in her community. I showered, shaved, put on a coat and tie, and looked presentable. Then I went to the early service at one church and the later service at the other. There was little or no greeting at either church when I arrived. At both, I sat in the middle of the congregation. No one sat near me. After worship, I joined the procession out past the clergy. People chatted all around me, but no one greeted me or engaged me in conversation. In each church the pastor greeted me briefly (which doesn't count because they're paid to do that). I went to both coffee hours, stood by myself drinking my lonely cup of coffee until I could stand it no longer and fled. Why would I ever return to either church? Yet those churches would claim they are each a friendly church.

After we accept that being hospitable is a requirement for being a Christian Church, we must proceed to make hospitality intentional and integral to our style and practice. Churches can announce to the world at large that they are a welcoming people through a newspaper ad, their sign board, a church Web site, flyers, letterhead, and word of mouth. A hospitable church reserves the best spot in the parking lot for visitors, makes its buildings handicap accessible, has clear signage directing the visitor to the front door and rest rooms, and adopts a statement of openness to all of God's people through policies such as being open and affirming as in my denomination. In San Rafael, we have at least one friendly person at the front door to welcome visitors and help them feel at home. Our goal is to make every visitor feel like a special guest. Guests are asked to sign our guest book, and each guest gets a personal welcoming letter from the pastor. They are given a written introduction to our church and a ball-point pen (with our name, address, and phone number) as a symbolic welcoming gift. Visitors are given a bulletin that's designed with them in mind and large print bulletins are available for the sight impaired and young readers.

The intent of our whole worship experience is, as Nouwen wrote, "to create the free and fearless space where brotherhood and sisterhood can be formed and fully experienced." This particularly happens during our time of greeting one another at the beginning, in the Assurance of Grace, the sermon (which always portrays the Christian faith and church as inclusive rather than exclusive), during our sharing of joys and concerns, and the passing of the peace at the end. It particularly happens on sacramental occasions. Marjorie J. Thompson, in her book, *Soul Feast*, expresses this idea beautifully: "In baptism, God opens the door to the family house and says, 'welcome home, my child!' In the Eucharist, God brings us to the dinner table and cries, 'Eat! Eat! I made it especially for you!'"[41] We seek to cement our hospitable welcome following worship by engaging our guests in conversation, ushering them to the refreshment table, connecting them with people of similar interests, and inviting them to return.

When we turned our traditional Christmas Eve service into a hospitality occasion by adapting the Hispanic La Pasada tradition, Mary, Joseph, and all our worshipers were cordially invited into the sanctuary to experience the hospitality of God and God's people. At the top of the bulletin was the greeting from a traditional La Pasada song: "Come in, holy pilgrims, accept this corner, not of this poor house, but of my heart. . . . This is a night of happiness, of joy and rejoicing, because we give hospitality here to the family and Son of God."

Each of us, all of us, live in a most inhospitable world. The Church, which is the Community of God, is an alternative and antidote to the hostile world. A story from the Hebrew tradition tells of the rabbi who asked his pupils how they could tell when the night had ended and the day had begun. One student answered, "Could it be when you can see an animal at a distance and can tell whether it's a dog or a sheep?" The rabbi said, "No, that's not how you can tell." "Could it be when you look at a tree at a distance and can tell whether it is a fig tree or a peach tree?" a student asked. "No," answered the rabbi. "Well, then, what is it?" the students demanded. "It is when you look on the face of any person and can tell that that is your brother or sister. Because if you cannot do this, then no matter what time it is, it is still night," said the rabbi. A church that does not exemplify a spirit of deep and universal hospitality is something other than a Christian church and is living in the darkness.

Questions:

1. When and where have you felt especially at home? And not at home?
2. How well and in what ways does your church welcome the alien, the stranger, the visitor and help them feel like an honored guest?

Suggestions:

1. Have three or four of your key leaders *go individually* to visit a church where they are completely unknown to experience how it is to be a stranger in a church and how another church does or does not extend hospitality.
2. Ask a discerning person to visit your church incognito and then come back to report to the appropriate group how she or he did and did not experience genuine hospitality in their midst. With all this data in mind, strategize together ways that your practice of hospitality can be strengthened, ways you can treat all visitors as the Christ.

FIVE

 CONCLUSION

What is the nature of the *search*? you ask.

Really it is very simple, at least for a fellow like me; so simple that it is easily overlooked.

The *search* is what anyone would undertake if he were not sunk in the *everydayness* of his own life. . . . To become aware of the possibility of the search is to be *onto* something. Not to be *onto* something is to be in despair [italics mine].[1]

—The Moviegoer

In Walker Percy's novel *The Moviegoer*, the main character, Binx Bolling, goes to the movies in his effort to search for what is really important in life. I, too, go to the movies, but it's in worship where I and others best engage in the search for the important, true, good, and holy. It's in worship where I and others transcend the everydayness of our own lives and discover a sense of community and meaning that enriches our living. It's in worship where that which I and others are onto is identified, defined, shared, and incarnated. It's in worship where the churches I know, first and best find their reason for being and doing.

I'm acutely aggravated that in both secular and religious circles, the value of what happens in the worship life and the rest of congregational life goes largely unrecognized and disrespected. To get noticed in either circle, a church must do something new or quirky, or commit some outrageous act, or engage in some activity that publicly impacts the community or world. In an effort to address this oversight, I preached a sermon that was an open letter to the Minister and President of the United Church of Christ. Here's what I said about worship.

Is there any human organization that has paid more dividends for God's purposes than churches? I don't think so.

Let's think about what happens in, through, and because of congregations. Start with the most important thing we do—worship. Each Sunday the six thousand UCC congregations, like a few hundred thousand other congregations, gather in cathedrals, sanctuaries, chapels, meeting rooms, and other worship settings to do that thing they call worshiping. Hopefully, God is not too offended at what we do in our efforts to praise the divine.

Beyond whatever value our worship has for God, imagine the cornucopia of value for the worshipers who are the congregation. We've heard it said that Sunday morning is the most segregated time of the week. To the contrary, I'm of the opinion that when America worships, it is more integrated than any other time. For example, when our little San Rafael church worships, we have several ethnic groups, the full range of economic groups, all ages, both genders, and the full range of political and theological viewpoints. And the miracle is we all care about each other, are getting to really know one another, and are a fair approximation of a Christian community. Every congregation I've served has been a beautiful mosaic in many ways. How precious and promising!

Most congregations sing a lot. Is there any place in American life where people sing more than in Christian worship? And we all know that music-making is wonderfully therapeutic and community building. Bonhoeffer was right that when the church sings, it is the whole Church singing together.

Most congregations pray more than once when they gather. They confess and give thanks. To do either moves the pray-ers out of their egocentric center and into relationship with both God and neighbor. When roughly one hundred million Americans pray each Sunday, it must be healthy and redemptive for the common good. They also pray for others. What is this worth? As we know, there's solid scientific documentation that prayer does, in fact, contribute to genuine healing and wholeness. I believe church folks find through their shared life, worship, and prayerful care giving a stronger will, reason, and power for living.

They generally hear the biblical and preached Word. Granted the scripture may be poorly chosen and read and the sermon is probably less than what God and the people in the pews desire. Martin Luther is supposed to have said, "God can carve rotten wood, ride a lame horse." If so, God can also touch people through a less than great sermon. Perhaps I'm deluded as a preacher, but I believe sermons probably do much more good than harm, and the general populace is better off for the efforts of its preachers.

And people do one more thing when they worship. Most of them give—money, as well as of themselves. It's well known that religious people are more generous than non-religious people and that people give far more in charitable contributions through their religious congregations than in any other way. Our little congregation of seventy mostly middle-class members will give over $100,000 to support the ministry and mission of their church this year, plus what they will give for the extensive capital improvements to our facility. They amaze me!

Is it exaggeration to suggest that the hour of worship is the most power-filled and influential hour of the week in America?

The introduction to this book began with T. S. Eliot's extraordinary claim:

What life have you if you have not life together?
There is no life that is not in community,
And no community not lived in praise of God.[2]

I have tried to demonstrate that smaller churches have the potential to fully realize Eliot's vision. They are the right size to be caring communities in which everyone is known and needed and plays a key role. They are the right size to praise God, to worship, to do the work of the people in authentic, transforming, and community building ways.

Twelve principles and fifteen practices have been offered which can enable any smaller congregation to worship in the most faithful and effective manner possible. A church that follows these principles and practices can expect to have size appropriate and spirited worship. This worship will likely lead to increased and more regular attendance, increased financial support, a happier and more productive congregation, and a heightened sense of mission beyond the doors of the church. Continuing to follow them will help your church maintain the qualities of smallness as it probably expands in size and service.

During World War I, the German U-boat submarines were creating terrible havoc among the Allied navies and threatening to bring the war to American shores. Humorist Will Rogers told a group how the Allies could eliminate the U-boats and win the war. He explained: "All the Allies have to do is boil the Atlantic Ocean. The increased pressure will pop the U-boats to the ocean surface where they will be sitting ducks for the Allied war ships. In a short time the war will be over." One exasperated listener responded: "But how in the world can the Allies boil the ocean?" Rogers answered: "I've given you the solution to the U-boat problem. I'm leaving it up to you to work out the details."

I've offered you, the reader, all the principles and practices you need to meet the liturgical needs and fulfill the worship possibilities of your smaller church. Better than Will Rogers, I've also provided a potpourri of ideas, strategies, and resources which grow out of real life experience. Now it's up to you and your people to work out the details in ways that are true to your history, theology, context, church personality, and particular size. By the grace of God and through worship created and enacted in ways appropriate and advantageous for your size, Christ will be experienced in your midst, just as he is when two or three gather in his name.

WORSHIP RESOURCES FOR SMALLER CHURCHES

The following resources have been used effectively by the author. They are included to stimulate the creativity of the reader as well as to serve as resources that may be used in their entirety or adapted for each individual. The author asks that credit be given and that the intent of the resources not be changed.

List of Resources

Is Our Worship the Worship of a Smaller Church? (A questionnaire)

Worship Survey

Preaching Survey

Guidelines for Worship Leaders

An Order of Worship: *The Art of Worship*

An Order of Worship: *Celebrating Smaller Churches*

Sermon on Worship: *Our Worship Is Our Offering*

Bible Study: *Gideon and the Midianites*

IS OUR WORSHIP THE WORSHIP OF A SMALLER CHURCH? (A QUESTIONNAIRE)

Background: This assessment tool would be best used along with a church's study of this book, but it could be used independently.

DIRECTIONS: There is a continuum for each Principle and Practice of smaller church worship. Please circle the number that best reflects your sense of your church's worship as it relates to each Principle and Practice. After finishing, add the circled numbers to determine how well your church fulfills the size-related possibilities for worship in smaller churches. The higher the number, the more faithful and effective your worship probably is.

Principle #1: Worship is about the worthiness of God and ourselves

Our worship is only a social, perfunctory gathering			Our worship focuses on God's holiness and our value		
1	2	3	4	5	6

Principle #2: Worship is the most important thing smaller churches do

Worship is the least important activity at our church			Our worship is our highest priority		
1	2	3	4	5	6

Principle #3: Smaller churches can worship very well

I would be embarrassed to have a visitor experience our worship			We think our worship is wonderful in every way		
1	2	3	4	5	6

Principle #4: Smaller churches are more likely to experience God as Immanent rather than as Transcendent (and they may prefer Jesus and the Holy Spirit)

To be honest, the whole idea of God doesn't mean much to us			God is at the very core of our living and our worship		
1	2	3	4	5	6

Principle #5: Much more happens when they come to worship than worship

We come, we worship, we go home—that's all			We connect, we worship, and many important things happen		
1	2	3	4	5	6

Principle #6: Their worship needs to be indigenous,
more than heterogeneous, and not homogeneous

Our worship could happen anywhere and doesn't fit our distinctiveness			Our worship grows out of who we uniquely are; is customized		
1	2	3	4	5	6

Principle #7: Most folks in smaller churches would
rather folk dance than watch a ballet

Most of us feel like spectators watching a performance			Most of us feel like we're personally involved in worship		
1	2	3	4	5	6

Principle #8: Smaller church worship is more
a public than a private experience

For most, worship is a private, isolated experience between God and each one			Our worship is communal and relates us to each other		
1	2	3	4	5	6

Principle #9: Worship in smaller churches is a family reunion

Most of us don't know or care about most of the others			We all know, are glad to see, and care about each other		
1	2	3	4	5	6

Principle #10: Small church worship is
a time for social caring and community building

Most of our folks care only about themselves			Worship helps us care and be more connected with each other		
1	2	3	4	5	6

Principle #11: Worship in small churches is more emotional

We never laugh or cry or express feelings in our worship			Laughter erupts, tears flow, emotions are felt in worship		
1	2	3	4	5	6

Principle #12: It's folly they don't like, not change

Our people don't want anything changed in their worship			We're open to variety and reasonable innovations		
1	2	3	4	5	6

BUILDING ON THESE PRINCIPLES, INCORPORATE THE FOLLOWING PRACTICES:

Practice #1: Design every part of smaller church worship for the number expected

The way we worship, it doesn't matter how many are present			Our worship is planned for and takes advantage of our size		
1	2	3	4	5	6

Practice #2: The order of worship matters

Our order of worship hasn't changed in years; no one cares			Our order is carefully planned; we prepare, hear, respond		
1	2	3	4	5	6

Practice #3: Worship the God who loves the remnant, the Jesus who turns water into wine, and the Spirit who refreshes and transforms us

The God we worship leaves us unmoved and unchanged			Our God loves us, our Jesus and Spirit restore and recreate us		
1	2	3	4	5	6

Practice #4: Design their worship as the work
of the people and the fruit of their gifts

In our worship, most watch what others do	Our worship involves us all and uses our gifts and talents		
1	2	3	4	5	6

Practice #5: Center smaller church worship on people not tasks

Our worship is impersonal and people are just cogs in the process	As we worship our people are needed and know they matter		
1	2	3	4	5	6

Practice #6: Make room for flexibility and spontaneity

We never depart from the fixed and planned way of doing things	We are free to respond to the Spirit and the unexpected		
1	2	3	4	5	6

Practice #7: Small churches want the song
they sing to be the song of their souls

We seldom sing the songs that we really love and move us	We love our music because it expresses ourselves and our faith		
1	2	3	4	5	6

Practice #8: Smaller churches need to
experience the scriptures as their own story

We glaze over or nod off when the scripture is read and used	When we use scripture, we feel it's about us and is our story		
1	2	3	4	5	6

Practice #9: The smaller church preacher is the folk dance caller

The sermon seldom awakens us and stirs us to response and action	The preacher motivates us to respond and act		
1	2	3	4	5	6

Practice #10: Worship should be seasonal,
celebratory, eventful, and keyed to life's stages

Our worship is essentially the same year-round			We celebrate the seasons and life's important events		
1	2	3	4	5	6

Practice #11: A house, people, and liturgy of prayer

Prayer is incidental to where we are, who we are, and what we do			Prayer is at the core of who we are and how we worship		
1	2	3	4	5	6

Practice #12: Customize the sacraments and
make them up-close and personal

Baptism, communion, sacramental events are also incidental to us			We anticipate the sacraments and they speak to and for us		
1	2	3	4	5	6

Practice #13: The worship space shapes the worship and the people

Our worship room leaves us cold and speaks to no one			Our space is beautiful, inspiring, and deepens our faith		
1	2	3	4	5	6

Practice #14: Worship so people leave
feeling healed, affirmed, equipped, and called

We go home feeling just the same as when we came			Our worship transforms us and equips us for the week to come		
1	2	3	4	5	6

Practice #15 Be a home of hospitality where
every visitor is a guest who wants to return

Visitors are free to like us or leave us; we don't care			We really try to make visitors feel welcome and at home		
1	2	3	4	5	6

Total Score_____

WORSHIP SURVEY

Introduction: You will help both your church and pastor if you take about fifteen minutes to fill out and return this survey. We need to understand how you experience worship in order to plan worship that will meet your hopes and needs. I, as your pastor, try to be thoughtful and intentional in planning worship, but that doesn't mean the worship I plan is as meaningful for you as it might be. What works and what doesn't work for you? Your candor in offering information, affirmation, and suggestions for improvement will be appreciated.

Some definitions may help you respond to this survey.
The word *worship* means to "grant worth to."
The word *liturgy* means "the work of the people."
My definition of worship is based on Jesus' Great Commandment. To me, *worship* is "the active response of the Christian community to God's love with the praises of our hearts, the yearnings of our souls, and the ponderings of our minds so that we are able to love one another and all of creation as we love ourselves."

Are you a . . .

_____ Frequent attendee here _____Visitor

If you are a regular attendee here, how many times a month do you attend:

_____ Four _____ Three _____ Two _____ Once

Ages:

_____Child/youth _____20 – 40 _____41 – 65 _____66 and older

*What is your denominational or religious background?*_____

What sizes of churches do you have significant experience in besides this one?

____Very small _____ Small _____ Medium _____ Large ____Very large

Would you prefer to worship with . . .

_____ Less than 50 _____ 50–100 _____100–200____200–500 ____More

Why do you prefer the size you indicated?

Why do you get yourself out of bed and choose to attend worship here?

Are your expectations generally met? Why or why not?

We worship at 10 A.M. Would you rather worship at

_____9:00 _____11:00 _____some other time? _____Why?

The pastor tries to keep worship to one hour. Does it bother you if worship runs 10–15 minutes longer?

_____Yes _____No. 15–30 minutes longer? _____Yes _____No.

The pastor spends considerable time on our order of worship or bulletin which results in more variety and requires more paper than you find in many church bulletins. Do you find our order of worship/bulletin . . .

_____ Interesting and _____ It's O.K. _____ Doesn't work for me.

Is our order of worship/bulletin . . .

_____ user friendly _____ confusing (if so why?).

Listed below are the elements of our worship experience.
Please use the following 5–1 scale to evaluate each:

5=Very meaningful; 4=Helpful; 3=O. K.; 2=Fair; 1 = Doesn't work for me

_____ Centering thoughts or quotes in bulletin

_____ Prelude music

_____ Welcome and Announcements

_____ Greeting each other

_____ Call to Worship

_____ Hymn choices/selection/way we sing them

_____ Time of Confession: Unison Prayer, Silent Prayer, Lord's Prayer,

_____ Assurance

_____ Children's Time

_____ Anthem(s), Introit

_____ Scripture(s)

Do we use too much or too little scripture? _____

_____Sermon

Are the pastor's sermons too long or too short? _____

Are they usually relevant to you? _____ *Interesting* _____

Suggestions for our preacher:

_____ Joys and Concerns and Pastoral Prayer

_____ Offering of Gifts

_____ Commission

_____ Passing of the Peace

_____ Postlude

We celebrate two sacraments in our church—Baptism and Communion.
Please evaluate using the 5–1 scale.

_____ The way we do baptisms in this church

_____ The way we practice communion here

Suggestions for either:

Do you have feedback about our celebration of the Church year
(Advent, Christmas, Lent, Easter, Pentecost)?

Would you like more or less lay participation in worship?

_____More _____Less

Please note kudos and suggestions for the pastor and lay participants:

For musicians and choir:

*Please note any hymns you'd like to sing **more** often:*

Less *often:*

Please note any guest preachers you'd like to invite or ask back:

Please note any improvements or changes that would make our sanctuary space work better for you or others:

Please note how we could make our Sunday gathering and worship more welcoming and attractive to visitors and new folks:

Please note any other suggestions on the back of this sheet. Sign your name if you're interested in talking with someone about our worship. Thank You for helping with this evaluation. Results will be shared. Please Return By: _____

PREACHING SURVEY

ntroduction: Thank you for being willing to give feedback to today's sermon and my preaching in general. Please comment briefly on the following. In addition to your written feedback, I invite you to converse with me about these matters. Again, thank your for your reactions! Please fill out and return to_____.Thanks again.

1. Preacher's Poise and Presence: (Note such things as posture, eye contact, use of notes, naturalness)

2. Preacher's Voice and Gestures: (Note projection and volume, clarity of diction, speech patterns, use of gestures and animation)

3. Preacher's Content: (Note whether sermon flowed out of and related to scripture; whether it related to your life and the world as you experience it; and whether it provided you with fresh insight or new understanding. Is there anything you are motivated to do in response to the sermon? If you can recall, please state the theme of the sermon in one phrase or sentence.)

4. Interest Level: (Note whether sermon held your attention—why or why not? Consider such things as imagery, stories and quotations, organization)

5. Basic Overall Impression:

6. What in particular do you like best about the preacher's preaching?

7. What in particular could the preacher do to strengthen his or her preaching?

8. If you can recall a favorite or significant sermon in the last year, what was it, and what made it so?

9. Is there a subject or biblical passage about which you would like the preacher to preach about this year?

Other comments:

GUIDELINES FOR OUR WORSHIP LEADERS

'm appealing to you to work with me in continually seeking to make our worship more faithful and effective. Another word for our order of worship is the *liturgy*. Liturgy means "the work of the people." You are crucial in seeing to it that our worship work is the best we can offer. Søren Kierkegaard compared worship to drama. He said that in the drama of worship, the pastor, lay leader, story teller, and the musicians are the prompters; the congregation are the actors; and God is the audience. As prompters or directors, **it is up to you and me** to see that all of our actors have the direction and help they need to act their part with power, purpose, and authenticity. In this spirit, here are some requests from your worship leader, the head prompter.

GREETER(S):

1. Be here and ready to greet by 9:30 (at the absolute latest).
2. We never have a second chance to make a first impression. You provide the first impression that visitors receive of our church. Being cordial and helpful to visitors and the recently arrived is your first and most important duty. Engage them in conversation. Get visitors' names and call them by name. Introduce yourself and our church and introduce visitors to others. Invite them to stay after worship for refreshments.
3. Show visitors the guest book and invite them to print their name and address. Give them the printed introduction to our church, a bulletin, and a newsletter.
4. If visitors are here with children, connect them with a church school teacher or another parent.
5. Be ready to orient visitors to the bathrooms, telephone, bulletin, hymnbook, and so on.
6. Be available to greet latecomers until about 10:10 and watch for others who may come after that.
7. Please count <u>ALL</u> worshipers, <u>including children</u>, and record the total on the attendance chart on the bulletin board.
8. Be attentive to visitors *after* worship, too. Do your best to see that visitors leave feeling like honored guests.

LAY LEADER OR READER:

1. Practice your parts out loud and in front of a mirror ahead of time so that you are not just reading words but communicating meaning and truth. Lead, don't just read.
2. Be seated before the prelude so that you can center and focus yourself. Visualize how you will be leading.
3. Practice the instructions out loud for standing and sitting, hymns, bulletin, praying the Lord's Prayer, and so forth. Confusion about standing and sitting is where we make the most mistakes. The reasons *those who are able* are invited to stand is as a sign of respect, to energize the worshiper, and so we can sing better. When there is an ⋆ in the bulletin, you are to say *Please stand if you are able.*
4. Speak directly into the microphone and make eye contact with worshipers so that all feel as though you're talking to them. Think of two or three people who do not hear well and speak with enough volume and clarity so that they can hear. If you cannot be heard, the word of God may not be heard.
5. If your leadership lacks energy and focus, the congregation's response will lack energy and focus.
6. As Lay Leader, you are not just a prompter, you are a *priest,* acting as an intermediary between worshiper and God and you are a *host* helping worshipers—especially visitors—feel welcome, safe, addressed, and at home.
7. The parts you lead are as important as the parts the pastor or preacher leads!

CHILDREN'S STORY TELLER:

1. All children are invited to the front, but don't embarrass those who don't come by insisting that they come.
2. Use the microphone so all can hear.
3. Keep your story or conversation with the children under five minutes.
4. If there are more than ten children, ask a teacher or parent to come help with noise and attention.
5. As much as possible, call the children by name so the children feel special and so the rest of the congregation can learn their names.
6. The purpose of the children's time is to help the children learn about and grow into the faith and to help them feel a part of the church community. The purpose is *not* to entertain the adults by helping the children say cute things.

7. Young children don't think in complex and abstract terms, so keep your language and ideas simple and concrete.
8. Try to keep what you communicate consistent with what our church believes and tries to practice.
9. If each child leaves feeling more known, loved, and related to our church and the Christian faith, you've really done your job. Thanks!

MUSICIANS:

1. Your role in worship is crucial. Well over 25 percent of our worship is music and if it's done well, our worship will work and transform. If it's done poorly, we've wasted a wonderful opportunity to touch and warm the collective heart of our people.
2. You are not performers, but music leaders for our congregation and co-leaders of worship. Thus, we look to you for guidance and inspiration.
3. Please help with punctuality. Finish your warming up, robe, and be in the sanctuary prepared to lead worship <u>before</u> 10:00. If you are alert and ready, the congregation will be, too.
4. Help eliminate dead time. Be ready. Have music in hand. Be purposeful. Stand together and sit together.
5. Be set up ahead of time. The middle of worship is not the time to arrange chairs, move the piano, put up a music stand, and so on.

USHERS:

1. Generally our greeters are our ushers. Know ahead of time who the other usher is and where the offering plates are. Be prompt in starting the offering.
2. It's good if there's variety in our ushers to reflect the variety in our church—old, young, female, male, newcomer, old timer.
3. To me, the times of Prayer and of Offering are the climax of the worship. The offering is far more than when we collect the money. Primarily, it's an opportunity for our people to offer their whole selves in response to God's love. Please communicate this deeper meaning by your demeanor and movement.

Thank you to all of you! Without you, our worship would be feeble and foolish. With you offering your best, it is faithful and effective. If you do your work well, our worship really will be the "work of the people."

AN ORDER OF WORSHIP:

THE ART OF WORSHIP

Background: The following order of worship was about the act of worship itself. Beside each element in the order of worship bulletin was an explanation of that element. The sermon "Our Worship Is Our Offering" is included in the sermons that follow. Use as much or as little of the order as you wish.

FIRST CONGREGATIONAL CHURCH (UCC)

July 11, 1999

The Art of Worship

Welcome to Our Worship! We come to worship, but why? What is it we do here? What do we hope for? How does it prepare us for and impact our living? The theme of our worship today is worship itself. You are invited to stand when you see an ★ in the bulletin.

Food for Thought:
What life have you if you have note life together?
There is no life that is not in community,
And no community not lived in praise of God.
—T. S. Eliot

Theologian Søren Kierkegaard compared worship to drama. He said that in true Christian worship the acting is done by the whole congregation. The prompters are the worship leaders and choir. The audience is God.

Continuing with the drama metaphor, true worship is a drama in three acts. **Act I** is when we prepare ourselves to come into God's presence by warming up, praising, confessing, and receiving the assurance of God's love and grace. **Act II** is hearing God's written, sung, and preached word. **Act III** is our responding with promises, intercessions, gifts, and accepting God's call to discipleship. The service begins when the worship ends. Now, let the actors be on stage and let the drama begin!

We Prepare (Act I)

LIGHTING OF THE CANDLES

The candles remind us that God brought light to a dark world and calls us to be light to the world.

PRELUDE

This is warm-up time. No actor or athlete can perform without it. Greet your co-actors, center yourself with prayer, study the hymns and prayers, let down your defenses, listen to the music, focus your attention.

WELCOME AND ANNOUNCEMENTS

Greeting and information sharing.

*COMMUNITY BUILDING

Individuals can meditate, but worship requires a community. Greet and connect with those around you.

*CHORAL INTROIT
"GATHERED HERE IN THE MYSTERY"

Become a people with one voice in the mystery through our singing.

*CALL TO WORSHIP

After being apart and going it alone, we are called to participate in a reunion of our family of faith and called to bring body, mind, and soul into God's presence for the purposes of praising our Creator and being recreated. Get ready and pay attention, so you don't miss your cue. Remember, you are literally being invited into God's very presence.

L: People of God, come with all your senses, with all that you are to worship the God who makes us one.

P: I have come to listen.

L: No! Come and HEAR the Word of God.

P: I have come to sniff.

L: No! come and INHALE the fullness of our common life.

P: I have come to nibble.

L: No! Come and PARTAKE fully of the goodness of God's love.

P: I have come to watch.

L: No! Come and SEE the vision God intends for the world.

P: I have come to be touched.

L: No! Come and FEEL the presence of the Holy Spirit.

★ HYMN FOR GATHERING "COME NOW, ALMIGHTY GOD"

Eph. 5:18–19. "Be filled with the Spirit, addressing one another in . . . hymns and spiritual songs, singing and making melody to the Lord with all your heart." Sing out!

UNISON PRAYER OF CONFESSION

Gracious God, we confess that which is always with us: broken places which seem never to mend, empty places which seem never to flower. Loving God, accept us and help us accept ourselves; lead us to those good and true things that are not compromised by anything within us. Mend us, fill us, help us bloom. Hear our prayers.

We can't worship until we've "come clean" of our pretenses before God. Remember that Jesus said that before we can worship we must first be reconciled with our brother or sister. Don't give God a laundry list of infractions, but tell God how you are, identify the pain and ruptures in your life. Forgive those you need to forgive.

SILENT PRAYERS OF CONFESSION

Silence isn't absence of activity, only absence of noise. Let God listen to your heart and mind.

THE LORD'S PRAYER

This prayer came to us from Jesus and binds us in solidarity with Christians of every time and place.

•ASSURANCE OF GRACE

This announces the miracle of faith that when we ask God to heal us and make us whole, God graciously does just that.

L: Paul assures us that there is absolutely nothing that can separate us from the Love of God. So let us praise God.

*HYMN OF GRACE, "AMAZING GRACE," VERSES 1 AND 3

This is the most extraordinary and joyful moment in our worship. Exult!

We Hear (Act II)

CHILDREN'S TIME

Here we honor our children, nurture them, and include them in our worship.

(Children may go to our summer children's program.)

ANTHEM

Our choir doesn't sing to perform or impress us, but to inspire us and lead our music. Since our choir is on vacation, we will all be the choir and sing one of your favorite hymns.

HEARING THE BIBLICAL WORD
Exodus 34:29–35
Luke 9:28–36

Worship grows out of and is centered in God's Word as discerned in scripture. Listen and ask what God is saying to us in our time.

SERMON
Our Worship Is Our Offering

Rather than being a monologue, the sermon is meant to be the first word of a dialogue. The preacher tries hard not to voice personal opinion, but to illuminate God's will for our living. A really good sermon will comfort the afflicted and afflict the comfortable.

We Respond (Act III)

Affirmation of Faith
A New Creed

The climax to the drama of worship is our response to God's love and word. Let us respond with truth and faith.

Time of Intercession and Prayer

Having been ministered to, we now begin to minister, holding in prayer those for whom and about which we have concern. We pray believing prayer changes things.

Joys and Concerns

Invitation to Prayer

L: Lift up your hearts.

P: We lift them up to the Lord.

Silent Prayers

Pastoral Prayer

The one praying out loud does not pray for us but leads us in praying.

Prayer Response

It's been said the one who sings prays twice. This is a sung prayer.

And God will raise you up on eagles' wings, bear you on the breath of dawn, make you to shine like the sun, and hold you in the palm of God's hand.

Offering of Gifts

It looks like this is a collection to support the ministry and mission of this church. In reality, this the offering of our whole selves to God and others.

Offertory

We receive the gift of music from one of our own.

*Doxology

This is the final climax to our worship. Grateful for the opportunity to worship and serve, we offer God our fervent praise with this ancient Judeo-Christian hymn.

Praise God from whom all blessings flow; Praise God all creatures here creatures here below; Praise God above, ye Heavenly Host; Creator, Christ, and Holy Ghost. Amen.

★HYMN OF SERVICE

"We Are Climbing Jacob's Ladder"

This is a marching hymn, an action hymn, meant to inspire and motivate. Sing with power and vigor.

★COMMISSION

These are our marching orders as we move from worship to service. It's like the act of commissioning a ship for its life at sea.

L: Go and share the good news

P: That God loves us all;

L: That in Christ, we have newness of life;

P: That the universe is good and exists on our behalf;

L: That life is full, both in joy and in struggle.

P: We go as a believing, serving people.

L: Go with the blessing of God the Creator, Redeemer, and Sustainer.

P: Amen and Shalom!

★PASSING OF THE PEACE

The Church has been greeting one another with the "Kiss of Peace" since its earliest days. Shake hands or hug, whatever is natural and welcome

★POSTLUDE

Music, not to cover the noise, but to usher you out to serve. Go in peace and come again.

AN ORDER OF WORSHIP:

CELEBRATING SMALLER CHURCHES

Background: The following worship service was designed to acknowledge, celebrate, and equip our smaller church for a productive ministry and mission, carried out without apology or excuse. It took place in the Easter season and expresses Easter themes.

FIRST CONGREGATIONAL CHURCH (UCC)

April 17, 1994

WELCOME TO THE THIRD WORSHIP OF EASTER when we stand in wonder at a God stronger than death who gives life that transcends assumed limits. Whether you are a guest, friend, or member, we're delighted that you're here. ★ marks the places where you're invited to stand.

For Your Reflection: The small church is not a pre-pubescent, immature, illigitimate, or malnourished large church. Because of its different size, it is a whole different species. It will look different, feel different, act different, be different.

—David Ray, *The BIG Small Church Book*

We Prepare

Lighting of Candles Acolytes

Prelude

Welcome and Announcements

★ First Call to Worship

Please welcome one another to our worship.

Choral Introit

★Second Call to Worship

L: Come, worship the Lord God who created all things, small and large.

P: Let us worship our Creator God.

L: Come, worship the Lord God who loves all churches, small and large.

P: Let us worship our Loving God.

L: Come, let us celebrate the smaller church and its crucial place in God's Good Plan.

P: Let us celebrate and renew ourselves for our important work as one of God's smaller and mighty churches.

★HYMN OF PRAISE

"O For a Hundred Tongues to Sing"
(We substituted "hundred" for "thousand.")

UNISON PRAYER OF CONFESSION

Loving God, creator of the atom, ant, and hummingbird: we've learned and often believed that small means puny, weak, and insignificant. Forgive us when we use our small size as an excuse for limited vision and weak action. Teach us again the biblical lessons of little David and Goliath, the leaven and the loaf, and the pearl of great price. Work and move among us as we worship and work together. Hear our excuses and confessions.

SILENT PRAYERS OF CONFESSION

★ ASSURANCE OF GRACE (FROM 1 COR. 1:26–30)

L: "Now remember what you were . . . when God called you. From the human point of view few of you were wise or powerful or of high social standing. God purposefully chose what the world considers weak in order to shame the powerful. God chose what the world looks down on and despises and thinks is nothing, in order to destroy what the world thinks is important."

P: By the grace of God "we are put right with God and we become God's only holy people and are set free."

★HYMN OF GRACE
"The Day of Resurrection "

We Hear

MINISTRY WITH CHILDREN (I USED *The Biggest House in the World* BY LEO LIONNI, A WONDERFUL CHILDREN'S BOOK ABOUT A SNAIL THAT IMAGINED HAVING A MUCH LARGER SHELL UNTIL IT REALIZED THE SHELL IT HAD WORKED BETTER.)

ANTHEM

SCRIPTURES: 1 SAMUEL 17:38; 50 AND JEREMIAH 31:7–8

*SERMON HYMN

"THIS LITTLE LIGHT OF MINE"

SERMON

"THE RIGHT SIZE"

We Respond

AFFIRMATION OF FAITH . . . IN GOD AND OURSELVES

L: Speak the words of Loren Mead:

P: **"We are enough, enough for faithfulness, enough for holding lives together and for making a contribution, enough for breaking bread and sharing wine, enough for wrestling with scriptures and for calling one another to life, enough for praying and following Jesus. We are enough!"**

SERVICE OF INTERCESSIONS AND PRAYERS

JOYS AND CONCERNS

L: Lift up your hearts.

P: **We lift them up to the Lord.**

SILENT PRAYERS, PASTORAL PRAYER, LORD'S PRAYER

CHORAL RESPONSE

OFFERING OF GIFTS

OFFERTORY

*Doxology

*Prayer of Dedication

*Hymn of Service

"I Sing a Song of the Saints of God"

*Commission

L: My people, take the message of 2 Kings 19:30–31 very seriously:
     "And the surviving remnant . . . shall again take root downward and
     bear fruit upward; for out of Jerusalem (and San Rafael and your
     town) shall go forth a remnant . . .a band of survivors.

P: **Let us thrust our roots deep in God's love and go bearing
     luscious fruit for a hungry world. Shalom until we meet
     again.**

* Passing of the Peace of Christ. Follow His Light into the World

* Postlude

SERMON ON WORSHIP:

OUR WORSHIP IS OUR OFFERING

Background: The following sermon was preached July 11, 1999, in San Rafael, in an effort to help this church explore the essential nature of worship.

SCRIPTURES: EXODUS 34:28–35 LUKE 9:28–37

Each Sunday, forty-five to sixty-five of us gather here when we could be in bed, at the beach, or in San Francisco. Why? What brings you here? Why are you here so regularly? For a few minutes I'd like for us to think about what we're doing right now. Think with a fresh spirit and inquiring mind about this thing we call "worship."

Worship is the most important thing churches do. If we don't worship well and faithfully, we won't be very good or faithful about the rest of our shared life. Quality worship is also crucial to quality living. When we don't worship well and faithfully, we shortchange both God and ourselves.

In Melville's *Moby Dick* there's a scene in which a small, open boat, a dory, moves across a turbulent sea in pursuit of the great white whale, Moby Dick. The sailors labor feverishly, every muscle taut; all attention focused on the task. Here's a parable that relates to the frenzy and conflict of our own lives.

In the dory, there's one sailor who appears to do nothing. He doesn't hold an oar, perspire, shout, or curse. He's braced in the bow, intent, poised, studying the water . . . waiting. Melville sees this as a metaphor for the rest of us: "To insure the greatest efficiency in the dart, the harpooners of this world must start to their feet out of idleness, and not from out of toil."[1]

In the same spirit, the Psalmist wrote, "Be still and know that I am God." And Isaiah wrote, "In returning and rest you shall be saved; in quietness and in trust shall be your strength."

The worship experience is like Melville's search for Moby Dick. We leave the security of home and port to search for that which our spirits hunger. The sailors hunger for the white, mythical whale. We hunger for God, for lasting love and meaning. In our search, and in the way we live, we're more like the frenzied sailors than the poised harpooner in the way we live.

Worship is *not* an easy or natural activity. And it's getting more difficult. Sunday used to be the primary coming together time of the community. People were more similar—large clans, similar nationalities and lifestyles, common religious background. People were dependent on the earth and

169

more subject to natural forces. God, faith, and church used to be central in people's lives—grace before meals, family devotions, worship every Sunday. Talk of God was part of daily conversation.

While life has changed dramatically, our needs and wants have not. We want to know who we are in the midst of this world. We need and want a sense of direction. We need and want to be part of a supportive community, connected by ties that bind. We need and want to love and be loved, to care for and be cared for. Deep down we know that life is more than consumption and compulsive activity. We need and want our lives to be more than the sum of our actions, more than three score and ten years of busyness. We want our lives to have an ultimate meaning and eternal assurance. The religious words for what we want is redemption and salvation. The existential words are meaning and purpose.

In Tennessee Williams's play, *Cat On a Hot Tin Roof*, Big Daddy describes our basic human search: "The human animal is a beast that dies and if he's got money he buys and buys and buys and I think the reason he buys everything he can buy is that in the back of his mind he has the crazy hope that one of his purchases will be life everlasting!"[2]

These are the fundamental questions that Christian worship addresses. And if these are our essentials, then worship ought to be number one on our list of weekly priorities, the place where one week ends and the next begins. Worship is to our lives as cultivation, fertilization, water, and light are to a garden. Weeds take over, nutrients are leached out, the soil becomes impacted, the roots can't spread. Cultivation opens up the soil so that food, water, and warmth can be absorbed by the plants so that growth and flowering can happen. Worship does this for us.

My definition of worship comes from Jesus' Great Commandment: Worship is the active response of the Christian community to God's love with the praises of our hearts, the yearnings of our spirits, and the ponderings of our minds, so that we are able to love one another and all of creation as we love ourselves. Christian worship is never a solitary experience. One person can meditate, but only a community of people can worship. Worship is a come-as-you-are party hosted by God. Worship is a three-act drama. We Prepare to be in God's and one another's presence, we Hear God's Word for our lives and world, and then we Respond to that Word, with the work of our lives.

Worship by definition is active, not passive; something we do, not something we observe. The word liturgy means "the work of the people," not the preacher. Theologian Kierkegaard described worship as a great drama in which the worship leaders are the prompters, the whole congregation are the actors on stage, and God is the audience in the pew. Churches tend to turn that around so that the minister, choir, and readers perform up front while the spectators sit back and watch the show. A yawn is stifled. The mind wanders to yesterday's experience or today's plan. The sermon is judged by whether it keeps us awake, entertains, and confirms or contradicts our pre-conceived notions. In this practice of worship God is either an after-thought or the recipient of mere lip service.

Consider what we mean when we use the word *worship*. Worship is the common and inclusive word for the life-creating occasions when the church gathers together as a community to express, explore, and commit to the faith that has brought them together. The word *worship* comes from the Old English word *weorthscipe* which literally means to give worth or respect to someone. We come to worship as an expression of the adoration and respect we have for God and to find greater worth in ourselves and our living. Worship is more of a verb than a passive noun. While King David danced before God, we too often simply sit back and watch.

Four principles, basic to the meaning of worship, guide my planning for our worship. First, I plan for our worship to have both a vertical and a horizontal dimension. Some people worship best in quiet as they approach God on a one-to-one basis. Other people best meet God through other people. God meets us both ways. In our worship, there's silent time when we're encouraged to open ourselves to God, listen carefully for God's stir-ring, leading to reconciliation with the source of our life. There's also both planned and spontaneous time when we meet each other and meet God through each other.

Second, there's an emphasis on our active participation in our worship. We might meditate privately and quietly, but we can only worship actively and in community. I prefer worship in small churches because everyone can be actively involved. Small church worship is like a participation game or a folk dance. Large church worship is like a spectator sport or a concert. While Jesus fed five thousand, he only gave the Lord's Supper to twelve.

Third, you'll find great variety in our worship, because variety is the spice of life. There's variety because I plan for the great diversity of religious backgrounds, personal tastes, and generations that are present. This also means that some things we do won't appeal to everyone's particular taste. Our worship has both formality and informality, variety of music, different forms of communication in sharing scripture and preaching, and flexibility in our sharing in the sacraments. And we have variety because my spiritual life has been enriched by the many diverse ways I've experienced worship around the world among different cultures and religious traditions.

Fourth, I work to make worship integral and concrete for the real lives that you live. Worship is often very other-worldly, full of pious, religious words which no longer communicate. I want our worship to be this-worldly because it's in this world where we all spend our time.

As we worship, take the structure of our Order of Worship seriously. We begin by Preparing, because you can't do anything important without preparation. Warm up always precedes athletic competition or the playing of a symphony. Come early. Greet one another. Come into the sanctuary in time to absorb the Prelude, pray the prayers of the bulletin and the hymns, pray for yourself and those around you. You can't worship without praising and expressing gratitude to the source of your life. You can't worship without dropping pretenses and opening yourself—as you are—to the one you are meeting here—which is confession. You can't worship without knowing you're the recipient of enormous portions of God's gracious graces. All this happens in our Preparing.

Worship requires Hearing. Why worship if we're closed to new wisdom, God's will and word to us which is revelation? Few people are really open minded and receptive in spirit. I pray we can be.

Worship requires Responding. The climax of our drama is when we respond with our sharing and intercessions, and when we respond with our offerings, including our financial investment in God's mission. We respond by accepting God's command to "go Ye into the world" to engage in ministry in our daily living.

Our consideration of our worship raises the question of the sacred space in which we worship. A worship room ought to communicate powerfully, even if nothing is sung, said, or done. A worship room ought to communicate what the people who worship there value and believe. A worship room ought to bring the Holy One and the worshiper closer together. A room where real worship happens changes simply by our being present in it. Few rooms that are called sanctuaries do this well How can our worship space be more conducive to what we want and need in our worship?

Phillips Brooks, composer of "O Little Town of Bethlehem" and famous pastor of Trinity Church in Boston, was teaching a preaching class. After enduring another dispirited sermon by a student, Brooks interrupted and asked, "Do you really expect every sermon you preach to change every one of your hearers?" The student stammered back, "Well not every one, every time." Brooks boomed back, "Well, that's your problem!" If we all come as regularly as possible, expecting something important to happen, and if we work to allow something important happen, important things will happen. If the sermon doesn't engage you, then let the hymns in the hymnal or the witness of the Bible, or a time of fervent prayer engage you. A poor sermon is not synonymous with poor worship. You and I are equally responsible for bringing quality, authenticity, and meaning to our worship. The proper question after every worship experience is not: What did I get out of it? Rather, it is: What did I put into it, how am I changed, and what will I do about it?

At an international worship service in Vancouver, British Columbia, worshipers were invited to come forward with a symbol of themselves as their offering. Everyone was touched and stunned when an African woman with a baby in arms came, placed the offering plate on the floor, stood over it, and said for all to hear: "I come and offer to God all that I have, my baby, and myself." Such an offering is the essence of authentic worship. That is our offering. Amen.

A BIBLE STUDY SERMON:
GIDEON AND THE MIDIANITES

Background: The following was taken directly from the *Today's English Version* of the Bible, edited a bit, and organized as a play script. (This can be done with many scriptures.) A worship leader/preacher might select a cast and use this as the scripture in worship and then preach about the story. Or the sermon following the dramatic reading might be a communal Bible study by the congregation, using the questions at the end of the play. Obviously, this story is highly relevant and encouraging for smaller congregations.

SCRIPTURE: Judges 6 and 7
(selected verses)

CAST: Narrator, Prophet, Angel/God, Gideon, and Everyone

NARRATOR: Once again the people of Israel sinned against the Lord, so he let the people of Midian rule them for seven years. The Midianites were stronger than Israel and the people of Israel hid from them in caves and other safe places in the hills. The Midianites would come with their cattle and tents, as thick as locusts. They and their camels were too many to count. They came and devastated the land, and Israel was helpless against them. Then the people of Israel cried out to the Lord for help against the Midianites, and the Lord sent them a prophet who brought them this message from the Lord, the God of Israel:

PROPHET: I brought you out of slavery in Egypt. I rescued you from the Egyptians and from the people who fought you here in this land. I drove them out as you advanced, and I gave you their land. I told you that I am the Lord your God and that you should not worship the gods of the Amorites, whose land you are now living in. But you have not listened to me.

NARRATOR: Then the Lord's angel came to the village of Ophrah and sat under the oak tree that belonged to Joash . . . His son Gideon was threshing some wheat secretly in a wine press, so that the Midianites would not see him. The Lord's angel appeared to him there and said:

ANGEL/GOD (sarcastically): The Lord is with you, brave and mighty man!

NARRATOR: Gideon said to him:

GIDEON (whining): If I may ask, sir, why has all this happened to us if the Lord is with us? What happened to all the wonderful things that our ancestors told us the Lord used to do—how he brought us out of Egypt? The Lord has abandoned us and left us to the mercy of the Midianites.

NARRATOR: Then the Lord ordered him:

GOD: Go with all your great strength and rescue Israel from the Midianites. I myself am sending you.

GIDEON (Continuing to whine): But Lord, how can I rescue Israel? My clan is the weakest in the tribe of Manasseh, and I am the least important member of my family.

GOD: You can do it because I will help you. You will crush the Midianites.

GIDEON: If you are pleased with me, give me proof that you are really the Lord.

NARRATOR: [Gideon then brought the angel meat and bread. The angel touched the food with a stick and it was burned up with fire which came from a rock. That night the Lord told Gideon to tear down his father's altar to Baal and replace it with an altar to the Lord your God. Gideon did and the people were furious with him.] Then all the Midianites, the Amalekites, and the desert tribes assembled, crossed the Jordan River, and camped in Jezreel Valley. The spirit of the Lord took control of Gideon, and he blew a trumpet to call the men of the clan of Abiezer to follow him. He sent messengers throughout the territory of both parts of Manasseh to call them to follow him. He sent messengers to the tribes of Asher, Zebulun, and Naphtali, and they also came to join him. [Gideon was still not quite sure, so he put the Lord to the test two more times.] The Lord said to Gideon:

GOD: The men you have are too many for me to give them victory over the Midianites. They might think that they had won by themselves, and so give me no credit. Announce to the people, "Anyone who is afraid should go back home, and we will stay here at Mount Gilead."

NARRATOR: So twenty-two thousand went back, but ten thousand stayed. Then the Lord said to Gideon:

GOD: You still have too many men. Take them down to the water, and I will separate them for you there. If I tell you a man should go with you, he will go. If I tell you a man should not go with you, he will not go.

NARRATOR: Gideon took the men down to the water, and the Lord told him:

GOD: Separate everyone who laps up the water with his tongue like a dog, from everyone who gets down on his knees to drink.

NARRATOR: There were three hundred men who scooped up water in their hands and lapped it; all the others got down on their knees to drink. The Lord said to Gideon:

GOD: I will rescue you and give you victory over the Midianites with the three hundred who lapped water. Tell everyone else to go home.

NARRATOR: So Gideon sent all the Israelites home, except the three hundred, who kept all the supplies and trumpets. The Midianite camp was below them in the valley. The Midianites, the Amalekites, and the desert tribesmen were spread out in the valley like a swarm of locusts, and they had as many camels as there are grains of sand on the seashore. The Lord told Gideon that if he was afraid to attack, he should sneak down into the enemy camp and hear what they were saying. He sneaked down and overheard a man describing a dream which suggested an Israelite victory. Gideon went back to the Israelite camp and said:

GIDEON: Get up! The Lord is giving you victory over the Midianite army!

NARRATOR: He divided his three hundred soldiers into three groups and gave each man a trumpet and a jar with a torch inside it. He told them:

GIDEON: When I get to the edge of the camp, watch me, and do what I do. When my group and I blow our trumpets, then you blow yours all around the camp and shout, "For the Lord and for Gideon!"

NARRATOR: Gideon and his one hundred men came to the edge of the camp a while before midnight, just after the guard had been changed. Then they blew the trumpets and broke the jars they were holding, and the other two groups did the same. They all held the torches in their left hands and the trumpets in their right, and shouted:

EVERYONE: **A sword for the Lord and for Gideon!**

NARRATOR: Every man stood in his place around the camp, and the whole enemy army ran away yelling. While Gideon's men were blowing their trumpets, the Lord made the enemy troops attack each other with their swords. They ran toward Zarethan as far as Beth Shittah, as far as the town of Abel Meholar near Tabbath.

Questions for Response and Discussion:

Introduce the reflection or Bible study on the story by saying the story is about what God expects of a faith community and how anything is possible when the community lives by faith.

1. Ask the actors how they felt as they played their parts.
2. Why was God angry with Israel? Do you see any parallels between then and now?
3. How did Gideon react to being drafted by God? Do we react in some of the same ways?
4. Why did God want Gideon to winnow or cut the troops from thirty-two thousand to three hundred? How does the world and church still operate as if bigger is better and might makes right? Can you think of illustrations of when smaller has been or could be advantageous?
5. Why did Gideon test God? How do we test God?
6. In addition to being empowered by God, what enabled Israel to prevail over the Midianites? (What did they do right?)
7. How does your church's story parallel this story? (Your sin? Your response to God's call? Your strategies? Your victories?)
8. If you were asked to preach on this story to this church, what would your sermon say?
9. Specifically and concretely—in the light of this story—what might we do as a church to live more faithfully and effectively?

NOTES

CHAPTER ONE

1. T. S. Eliot, "Choruses from 'The Rock,'" *The Complete Poems and Plays, 1909–1950* (San Diego: Harcourt Brace Jovanovich, 1950), 101–02.

2. Tom F. Driver, *Liberating Rites: Understanding the Transformative Power of Ritual* (Boulder, Col.: Westview Press, 1998), 5.

3. Robert Fulghum, *From Beginning to End: The Rituals of Our Lives* (New York: Villard Books, 1995), frontispiece.

4. Katie G. Cannon et al. [Mud Flower Collective], *God's Fierce Whimsy: Christian Feminism and Theological Education* (New York: The Pilgrim Press, 1985), 178.

5. Driver, *Liberating Rites*, 31.

6. Carl S. Dudley, "Old and New Unite in Ritual," *The Christian Ministry* (Jan.–Feb. 1998): 9.

7. Horace T. Allen Jr., "Liturgy as the Form of Faith," *The Landscape of Praise: Readings in Liturgical Renewal*, ed., Blair Gilmer Meeks (Valley Forge, Penn.: Trinity Press, 1966), 8.

8. James F. White, *Introduction to Christian Worship* (Nashville: Abingdon, 1980), 31f.

9. Ibid., 33.

10. Annie Dillard, *Holy the Firm* (New York: Harper & Row, 1984), 55–59.

CHAPTER TWO

1. Kirkpatrick Sale, *Human Scale* (New York: Coward, McCann & Geoghegan, 1980), 60.

2. Lyle E. Schaller, *Looking in the Mirror: Self-appraisal in the Local Church* (Nashville: Abingdon Press, 1984), 15–23.

CHAPTER THREE

1. William H. Willimon and Robert L. Wison, *Preaching and Worship in the Small Church* (Nashville: Abingdon Press, 1980), 26.

2. Kathleen Norris, *Dakota: A Spiritual Geography* (New York: Ticknor & Fields, 1993), 133.

3. David R. Ray, *The Big Small Church Book* (Cleveland: The Pilgrim Press, 1992), 69.

4. One of the best sources of information regarding the healing properties of religious faith is Larry Dossey's book *Healing Words: The Power of Prayer and the Practice of Medicine* (San Francisco: HarperSanFrancisco, 1993). See also Claudia Wallis, "Healing: A Growing and Surprising Body of Scientific Evidence Says They Can," *Time*, 24 June 1996, 59–62.

5. Dudley, *Making the Small Church Effective* (Nashville: Abingdon Press, 1978), 44–45.

6. Fulghum, *From Beginning to End*, 260.

7. Nancy T. Ammerman, "Culture and Identity in the Congregation," *Studying Congregations: A New Handbook*, ed. Nancy T. Ammerman et al. (Nashville: Abingdon Press, 1998), 84.

8. Dudley, *Making the Small Church Effective*, 36–37.

9. Patch Adams, *Gesundheit!: Bringing Good Health to You, the Medical System, and Society through Physician Service, Complementary Therapies, Humor, and Joy*, with Maureen Mylander (Rochester, Vt.: Healing Arts Press, 1993), 104.

10. Ibid., 92.

11. Dudley, *Making the Small Church Effective*, 35.

12. Ibid., 48.

13. Adams, *Gesundheit!*, 99.

14. Fulghum, *From Beginning to End*, 55.

15. Ray, *The Big Small Church Book*, 61.

16. Roy Rappaport, *Ecology, Meaning, and Religion* (Berkeley: North Atlantic Books, 1979), 49.

17. John H. Westerhoff III, *Bringing Up Children in the Christian Faith* (Minneapolis: Winston Press, 1980), 21.

18. Elie Wiesel, *Souls on Fire: Portraits and Legends of Hasidic Masters*, trans. Marion Wiesel (New York: Random House, 1973), 257

19. Paul D. Hanson, *The People Called: The Growth of Community in the Bible* (San Francisco: Harper & Row, 1986), 1, 5–6.

20. Dietrich Bonhoeffer, *Life Together*, trans. John W. Doberstein (New York: Harper & Row, 1954), 21.

21. Elizabeth O'Connor, *The New Community* (New York: Harper & Row, 1976), 58.

22. Eliot, "Choruses from 'The Rock,'" 101-02.

23. *The New Century Hymnal* (Cleveland: The Pilgrim Press, 1995), 775.

24. Driver, *Liberating Rites*, 156.

CHAPTER FOUR

1. Ray, *The Big Small Church Book*, 28.

2. Clark Saunders and Clair Woodbury, *Ministry as an Art* (Etobicoke, Canada: The United Church Publishing House, 1996), 10.

3. Benjamin Griffin, "The Choreography of Worship: Script, Music, Space, Movement," *Today's Ministry* 15, no. 2 (1998): 2.

4. Frank C. Senn, "The Spirit of the Liturgy, A Wonderland Revisited," in *The Landscape of Praise: Readings in Liturgical Renewal*, ed. Blair Gilmer Meeks (Valley Forge, Penn.: Trinity Press International, 1996), 18.

5. Elizabeth O'Connor, *Eighth Day of Creation: Gifts and Creativity* (Waco, Tex.: Word Books, 1971), 13.

6. Bonhoeffer, *Life Together*, 94.

7. Loren Mead, "Judicatory Interventions Can Help Small Congregations," in *New Possibilities for Small Churches*, ed. Douglas Alan Walrath (New York: The Pilgrim Press, 1983), 87.

8. Dudley, *Making the Small Church Effective*, 70.

9. Ibid., 48.

10. Norris, *Dakota*, 91.

11. White, *Introduction to Christian Worship*, 109.

12. Miriam Therese Winter, *Preparing the Way of the Lord* (Nashville: Abingdon Press, 1978), 78.

13. Bonhoeffer, *Life Together*, 60–61.

14. Gerard S. Sloyan, "What Is Liturgical Preaching?" in *The Landscape of Praise*, 232.

15. Anthony Trollope, *Barchester Towers*, introd. William Targ (Cleveland: Fine Editions Press, 1952), 252; 426.

16. White, *Introduction to Christian Worship*, 157.

17. Reuel L. Howe, *Partners in Preaching: Clergy and Laity in Dialogue* (New York: Seabury Press, 1967), 43.

18. John R. Claypool, *The Preaching Event* (Waco, Tex.: Word Books, 1980), 36.

19. Fred B. Craddock, *Preaching* (Nashville: Abingdon Press, 1985), 24–25.

20. Jay Weener, "A Word from Jay Weener," *Reformed Review* 44 (autumn 1990), 3–4.

21. Sloyan, "What is Liturgical Preaching?" 228.

22. Henri J. M. Nouwen, *Creative Ministry* (Garden City, N.Y.: Doubleday, 1971), 35–39.

23. Norris, *Amazing Grace: A Vocabulary of Faith* (New York: Riverhead Books, 1998), 180–81.

24. Fulghum, *From Beginning to End*, 254.

25. Don E. Saliers, *Worship as Theology: Foretaste of Glory Divine* (Nashville: Abingdon Press, 1994), 118.

26. Norris, *The Cloister Walk* (New York: Riverhead Books, 1996), 280–81.

27. Patricia Wilson-Kastner, *Sacred Drama: A Spirituality of Christian Liturgy* (Minneapolis: Fortress Press, 1999), 5.

28. Driver, *Liberating Rites*, 209, 211.

29. Westerhoff, *Liturgy and Learning Through the Life Cycle* (New York: Seabury Press, 1980).

30. Willimon, *Sunday Dinner: The Lord's Supper and the Christian Life*, introd. John Westerhoff III (Nashville: The Upper Room, 1981), 107.

31. Westerhoff, *Bringing Up Children in the Christian Faith*, 1980), 3f.

32. Wilson-Kastner, *Sacred Drama*, 129f.

33. Mircea Eliade, *Patterns in Comparative Religions*, trans. Rosemary Sheed (New York: Sheed and Ward, 1958), 367–69.

34. Dudley, *Making the Small Church Effective*, 95.

35. Gilbert Frederick Cope, ed., *Making the Building Serve the Liturgy: Studies in the Reordering of Churches* (London: A. R. Mowbray, 1962), 5.

36. Ray, *The Big Small Church Book*, 66.

37. Cope, *Making the Building Serve the Liturgy*, 5.

38. Nouwen, *Creative Ministry*, 102.

39. Marjorie J. Thompson, *Soul Feast: An Invitation to the Christian Spiritual Life* (Louisville: Westminster John Knox Press, 1995), 54.

40. Nouwen, *Reaching Out: The Three Movements of the Spiritual Life* (Garden City, N.Y.: Doubleday & Company, 1975), 46.

41. Thompson, *Soul Feast*, 124f.

CHAPTER FIVE

1. Walker Percy, *The Moviegoer* (New York: Alfred A. Knopf, 1961), 13.

2. Eliot, "Choruses from 'The Rock,'" 101.

RESOURCES

1. Herman Melville, *Moby Dick* (Norwalk, Conn.: Eaton Press, 1997), 308.

2. Tennessee Williams, *Cat on a Hot Tin Roof* (New York: New Directions Publishing, 1975), 91.

BIBLIOGRAPHY

Bonhoeffer, Dietrich. *Life Together*. Trans. John W. Doberstein. New York: Harper & Row, 1954.

Claypool, John R. *The Preaching Event*. Waco, Tex.: Word Books, 1980.

Craddock, Fred B. *Preaching*. Nashville: Abingdon Press, 1985.

Dawn, Marva J. *Reaching Out without Dumbing Down: A Theology of Worship for the Turn-of-the-Century Culture*. Grand Rapids, Mich.: William B. Eerdmans Publishing Company, 1995.

Dillard, Annie. *Holy the Firm*. New York: Harper & Row, 1977.

Doran, Carol and Thomas H. Troeger. *Trouble at the Table: Gathering the Tribes for Worship*. Nashville: Abingdon Press, 1992.

Driver, Tom F. *Liberating Rites: Understanding the Transformative Power of Ritual*. Boulder, Colo.: Westview Press, 1998.

Dudley, Carl S. *Making the Small Church Effective*. Nashville: Abingdon Press, 1978.

Fulghum, Robert. *From Beginning to End: The Rituals of Our Lives*. New York: Villard Books, 1995.

Hanson, Paul D. *The People Called*. San Francisco: Harper & Row, 1986.

Hellwig, Monika. *The Eucharist and the Hunger of the World*. Franklin, Wisc.: Sheed & Ward, 1999.

Humphrey, Caroline and Piers Vitebsky. *Sacred Architecture*. Boston: Little, Brown, and Company, 1997.

Lebacqz, Karen. *Word, Worship, World, and Wonder: Reflections on Christian Living*. Nashville: Abingdon Press, 1997.

Lionni, Leo. *The Biggest House in the World*. New York: Pantheon, 1968. A beautiful picture book; good for children's stories.

Meeks, Blair Gilmer, ed. *The Landscape of Praise: Readings in Liturgical Renewal*. Valley Forge, Penn.: Trinity Press International, 1996.

Norris, Kathleen. *The Cloister Walk*. New York: Riverhead Books, 1996.

———. *Dakota: A Spiritual Geography*. New York: Ticknor & Fields, 1993.

Nouwen, Henri J. M. *Reaching Out: The Three Movements of the Spiritual Life*. Garden City, N.Y.: Doubleday & Company, Inc., 1975.

O'Connor, Elizabeth. *Eighth Day of Creation: Gifts and Creativity*. Waco, Tex.: Word Books, 1971.

Percy, Walker. *The Moviegoer*. New York: Alfred A. Knopf, 1961.

Ray, David R. *The Big Small Church Book*. Cleveland: The Pilgrim Press, 1992.

———. *Small Churches Are the Right Size*. New York: The Pilgrim Press, 1982.

Sale, Kirkpatrick. *Human Scale*. New York: Coward, McCann, & Geoghegan, 1980.

Saliers, Don E. *Worship as Theology: Foretaste of Glory Divine*. Nashville: Abingdon Press, 1994.

Saunders, Clark and Clair Woodbury. *Ministry as an Art*. Etobicoke, B.C.: The United Church Publishing House, 1996.

Schaller, Lyle E. *The Small Church Is Different!* Nashville: Abingdon Press, 1982.

Thompson, Marjorie J. *Soul Feast: An Invitation to the Christian Spiritual Life*. Louisville: Westminster John Knox Press, 1995.

Wagley, Laurence A. *Preaching with the Small Congregation*. Nashville: Abingdon Press, 1989.

Westerhoff, John H. III. *Bringing up Children in the Christian Faith*. Minneapolis: Winston Press, 1980.

——. *Will Our Children Have Faith?* New York: Seabury Press, 1976.

White, James F. *Introduction to Christian Worship*. Nashville: Abingdon Press, 1990.

Willimon, William H., and Robert L. Wilson, *Preaching and Worship in the Small Church*. Nashville: Abingdon Press, 1980.

Wilson-Kastner, Patricia: *Sacred Drama: A Spirituality of Christian Liturgy*. Minneapolis: Fortress Press, 1999.